PENGUIN BOOKS

CONTROL YOUR OWN SUPER FUND

Paul Clitheroe AM has been a leading media commentator for more than 30 years, and is chairman and chief commentator at *Money* magazine. He is a founding director of the financial-planning firm ipac and was recently made a life member of the Securities Institute. He is past president of the Financial Planning Association, a council member of Philanthropy Australia and the chairman of the Australian Government Financial Literacy Board and the Australian String Quartet. Paul's book *Making Money* is a bestseller, and he was made a Member of the Order of Australia in 2008. He lives in Sydney with his wife Vicki.

Peter Crump is an actuary and financial adviser specialising in superannuation. He is a Fellow of the Institute of Actuaries of Australia and a Chartered Tax Adviser, and is Vice Chairman of SPAA, the SMSF Professionals' Association of Australia. Peter currently works at ipac south australia. He is a regular presenter to industry forums on superannuation, and is regarded as one of Australia's leading experts on self-managed super funds.

CONTROL YOUR OWN SUPER FUND

Paul Clitheroe

with Peter Crump

PENGUIN BOOKS

PENGUIN BOOKS

Published by the Penguin Group
Penguin Group (Australia)
707 Collins Street, Melbourne, Victoria 3008, Australia
(a division of Penguin Australia Pty Ltd)
Penguin Group (USA) Inc.
375 Hudson Street, New York, New York 10014, USA
Penguin Group (Canada)
90 Eglinton Avenue East, Suite 700, Toronto, Canada ON M4P 2Y3
(a division of Penguin Canada Books Inc.)
Penguin Books Ltd
80 Strand, London WC2R 0RL England
Penguin Ireland
25 St Stephen's Green, Dublin 2, Ireland
(a division of Penguin Books Ltd)
Penguin Books India Pvt Ltd
11 Community Centre, Panchsheel Park, New Delhi – 110 017, India
Penguin Group (NZ)
67 Apollo Drive, Rosedale, Auckland 0632, New Zealand
(a division of Penguin New Zealand Pty Ltd)
Penguin Books (South Africa) (Pty) Ltd
Rosebank Office Park, Block D, 181 Jan Smuts Avenue, Parktown North, Johannesburg, 2196, South Africa
Penguin (Beijing) Ltd
7F, Tower B, Jiaming Center, 27 East Third Ring Road North, Chaoyang District, Beijing 100020, China

Penguin Books Ltd, Registered Offices: 80 Strand, London WC2R 0RL, England

First published by Penguin Group (Australia), 2013

10 9 8 7 6 5 4 3 2 1

Text copyright © Paul Clitheroe Communications Pty Ltd 2013

The moral right of the author has been asserted

Cover and text design by Marley Berger © Penguin Group (Australia)
Cover photograph Andy Roberts/Getty Images
Typeset in 11pt Chaparral Pro by Penguin Design Studio
Printed and bound in Australia by McPherson's Printing Group, Maryborough, Victoria

National Library of Australia
Cataloguing-in-Publication data:

   Clitheroe, Paul.
   Control your own super fund / Paul Clitheroe.
   9780670077359 (paperback)
   Pension trusts--Australia.
   Investments--Australia.
   Retirement--Planning--Australia.
   Retirement income--Australia.
   Finance, Personal--Australia.

   332.672530994

penguin.com.au

Contents

INTRODUCTION

Weighing up superannuation

The rules governing superannuation keep changing, which is a source of frustration to many. Australians in general are not as inclined as citizens of other countries to a good conspiracy theory but the fact is change rattles people's cages, and I am asked on a regular basis if future governments will keep changing the rules, tax super out of existence or just steal it. My answer to these three questions is yes, no and no.

Australia has well over one trillion dollars in super today, and it will grow to many trillions very quickly. Any government has reason to be excited about this treasure trove and its potential to be taxed, or to be directed into investments that suit the government such as infrastructure, new roads, bridges and so on. It would be naive to think that future governments will not look at this vast pot of money and want a say in it. We have seen big changes lately with the maximum tax-deductible amount most of us can contribute restricted to $25 000 a year.[1]

---

1 Higher limits apply for those over age 59 in the 2013/2014 financial year and for those over age 49 in the 2014/2015 financial year.

The introduction of this restriction is no great surprise. The reality is that the biggest benefits in super belong to the highest taxpayers. If you are paying around 47% tax on your income, the ability to pay 15% on money going into super is like a gift from the heavens. But it makes the number-crunchers in government uneasy, reasoning that you have just quite legally avoided around 32% in tax. They argue this money could go to roads and schools. You argue the government will just waste it and it is better that you put it into super so you can live without government support at retirement.

In fact, both you and the number-crunchers have a valid argument. I suspect you are both correct, and are never going to agree. But like it or not, for good reasons or bad, successive governments will play with our super for what they believe are very good social, community and policy objectives.

One change I will foreshadow, and agree with, is a limit on how much tax-free super we can access at retirement when we are over 60. The idea that we can pop money into super at a 15% tax rate, enjoy a maximum 15% tax on earnings inside super, then retire after 60, take the lot tax free, pay off our debts, buy a car, take a holiday and then put out our hand for a pension is actually quite ridiculous. The notion of legally avoiding tax while we are working may be appealing, but the objective of superannuation is to allow us to reduce our tax to build up money that we then gradually use in retirement – basically, it is our own personal pension scheme. The more money we whack into super, the bigger our personal pension – and the better lifestyle we can afford. That actually makes sense. So expect in time to come that a fair chunk of our super will be legislated to stay in super for us to draw out to live on. That saves the aged-pension system money and makes the tax break we get a fair deal.

So the bad news is that yes, we are going to see more changes to the laws governing super. Some we will agree with; some we will hate. Some we will not like because they do not suit us, but we won't be too cranky because the changes may actually be fair to our community, if not to us personally.

The good news is that no government will tax super out of existence, or steal it. Let's think about these two conspiracy theories. Neither overtaxing super nor simply pinching it is going to work in a democracy. No political party would get away with it, for a start. And even under a dictatorship, stealing super makes no sense. If a government takes our savings from us, then that government will have to support us.

For any government, super is a balancing act. It makes sense on a number of levels to have us putting some of our pay aside to pay for our future lifestyle plans. It also makes sense to make this compulsory, or most of us just won't do it. Then to add some incentive in the form of tax breaks to make us feel positive about our superannuation scheme, and to encourage us to put in a bit more, is good economic management and sound government.

History of superannuation in Australia

Super has been around for longer than most people may think, and even before it came into existence the principles that underpinned its early forms were very old. Some form of benefit to long-serving employees has been around for ages, and in Australia, records from the 19th century show that companies and the public sector often had some form of payment or pension to reward long service. The paid workforce was mainly men, and with male life expectancy well below 60 years in the 1800s I doubt this was a large cost to government or industry.

Let's take a look at a chronology of events related to super:

1908: Invalid and Old Age Pensions Act is passed, paying 26 pounds a year to eligible men and women aged over 65

1910: Women's age for pension reduced to 60

1912: Family home removed from aged pension test

1915: Employer contributions to super become tax deductible

1961: Super funds exempt from tax if they hold Commonwealth Bonds

1972: 32% of workers covered by super

1975: Age pensions linked to 25% of average weekly earnings

1977: Fraser Government rejects a compulsory super scheme

1983: Hawke Government expresses support for employee super

1984: Age pension assets test introduced

1986: Australian Labor Party and ACTU seek 3% compulsory super

1987: Super funds top $41 billion

1998: 51% of employees covered by super

1992: Compulsory super starts

1993: 72% of employees covered by super

1995: Super funds reach $187 billion

1996: Treasurer Peter Costello introduces 'super surcharge' tax

1997: 81% of employees covered by super

1998: CGT on super funds reduced to 10%

2002: Compulsory contributions move to 9%

2003: Government co-contributions for low-income earners introduced

2004: Employee 'choice of super' introduced

2005: Super surcharge abolished

2006: Simpler Super announced, no tax on lump sums

2007: The largest super funds exceed $1 billion in assets

2009: Rate of co-contributions are lowered

2009: Limit on concessional contributions reduced

2010: Cooper's 'My Super' report released

2012: Proposal to tax contributions at 30% for higher-income earners

2013: Compulsory super contribution first increase for a while, on its way from 9% to 12% (by 2019)

As you can see, superannuation has undertaken quite an evolution. But there has been no sign of tax destroying super, or of governments trying to pinch it.

Are there better ways to save?

Whether or not super is the most effective way to save for retirement is a very valid and sensible question. The disadvantage of saving through super is the plethora of rules and rule changes that are sure to come. The advantage lies purely in the tax breaks.

Compulsory superannuation contributions are now in excess of 9%. There's little point arguing over this as a method of saving, as we have no choice in the matter. It makes sense though for the 12 million or so of us who have superannuation to at least take a minimal amount of interest and make sure we are in a decent, low-cost fund and that we are not paying for things we do not need. For example, a super fund is a good place to buy insurance, but only if you need it. But is super the place to put your voluntary savings?

The answer here depends a lot upon your age, your tax rate and your attitude to risk. As I write this, I am 58, I pay maximum tax on the top part of my income and in my pre-retirement stage of life I don't really fancy taking on large debts to fund investments.

I am a lower risk-taker than I used to be – in fact I am increasingly moving towards wealth preservation. So for me, super is an attractive proposition. I can contribute voluntarily $25 000 from my salary via salary sacrifice. On this $25 000 I pay 15% tax, so I end up with $21 250 in my super fund to invest in property, shares, fixed interest or whatever. But if I take my $25 000 in pay, I end up with around $13 250 after tax. I do not need to be Albert Einstein to realise that $21 250 invested is going to make me a lot richer than $13 250 invested. In fact, I'll need to earn some 60% after tax on the money in my pocket just to catch up to the amount in my super fund, even if it earns nothing.

The other risk factor that diminishes with age is the government messing around with the rules. In a couple of years at age 60, I could technically retire, turn my super fund into a tax-exempt vehicle on earnings and pull out lumps of money tax free whenever I like. For me, super is a no-brainer.

But for each of my three children, who are aged between 18 and 25, super is not so flash as a place for voluntary saving. Firstly, they are quite low taxpayers, so the difference between their personal tax rate and the 15% tax going into super is not terribly remarkable. Secondly, while I am not a conspiracy theorist, retirement for them is many decades away. Who knows what will happen over 40-plus years. Finally, they all like the idea of owning a house or apartment, so for them about the best deal going is the government's first home saver account – where your balance is increased by a contribution from the government, up to a limit each year if you qualify. What's more, you only pay 15% tax on the interest the account earns.

The first home saver account is beyond the scope of this book, but let me complete this line of thought. The older you are, the higher your taxable income and the more comfortable you are with lower risk due to no borrowings, the more super will appeal. You can borrow with your own super fund to buy property, which changes the risk picture a lot – we come to this in Chapter 7 – but right now, let's keep focused on the principles.

Interestingly, not only can you invest pre-tax earnings into super, and claim a tax deduction on your super if you are self-employed – you can also whack in a big lump of your own cash. The reasons for doing this follow the logic above. I think it is a terrific idea for me, but a shocker for my kids. You see, anyone can put $150 000 of their own after-tax money into super every year. You can also contribute the equivalent of three years of this in one year (with no contributions in the following two years). That's $450 000. This is fabulous for someone in my position because my fund only pays 15% tax on investment income and 10% on capital gains on investments held over a year.

But if my kids won lotto, my advice would be not to put the winnings into super – I would see that amount as a fair chunk of a home to live in or as an investment.

Where does super 'fit' in my planning?

Well, so far we have really only looked at the two extremes of super, using my young adult kids and my own situation as examples. Clearly for me super is just a brilliant option because of my age, my level of personal tax, my conservative attitude to risk and my future lifestyle plans.

But at the other extreme, for my low-tax-paying kids, with decades to retirement and a broad plan to own a property, apart from the compulsory super (increasing to 12%), investing extra money into super is not the best thing for them at this stage in their lives.

Extremes are nice and easy – the answer tends to be an absolute yes or no. But I suspect that most readers are likely to be less certain about whether additional super is the best option, and if it is, the question is how do you run your super most effectively? Is the right answer an industry fund, a retail fund, or do you set up your own do-it-yourself super fund?

The starting point is not about super – it is about you and your plans. How much money will you need? If we can sort out where you are now and what you want to achieve in the future, your decision in regard to the whys and hows of super will become a lot clearer.

CHAPTER 1

How much is enough?

In my role as a financial adviser I find I get frustrated by questions about whether super is any good, should I start my own DIY fund, negatively gear a property or buy shares. Another popular one is to ask for a hot tip. By this I think people are looking for a property or a share that will double or triple in value. If I actually knew this, why would I be writing this book? Personally I think the best question for a so-called financial expert is 'Why are you working?' If we so-called experts could actually pick property and share markets we would not need to work. In fact, now I think about it, I've yet to meet a rich economist, so clearly we 'experts' do not possess too many reliable 'hot tips'.

If you are absolutely desperate to get your own DIY fund going, ignore this chapter and go straight to Chapter 3. However, a warning that while starting a DIY fund may be right for you, this is the part of the book that will help you to create wealth. A DIY fund is simply one of the tools at your command once you know what you are aiming at.

Let's start at the end – well, maybe not quite the very end. The end I have in mind is a goal, and that goal for all of us is not retirement. 'Retirement' is a silly, old-fashioned word, better used in the days when we stopped working at 65 and died a few years later. At least then it was realistic, and for a couple of reasons.

Firstly, the fewer the number of years between when you stop work and when you die, the less money you need. So retiring at around 65 and then dying within five to 10 years of stopping work was quite a realistic financial proposition for most of us. Surviving for half a decade or so is very possible without a heap of money. Secondly, retirement not many decades ago meant pottering around the garden, a bit of golf and maybe a cheap meal out, so an aged pension and a small retirement nest egg was all that was needed even if you did outlive the average life expectancy.

But both of these prerequisites that made retirement a sensible proposition for many of us have fundamentally changed. The first change is that we are clearly, on average, living longer – a lot longer. In the early 1900s, shortly after the start of our aged pension system, we had a male qualifying age of 65 and 60 for females. This made a lot of sense. Life expectancy, from birth, in 1908 was 54 for males and a few years more for females. So the typical male worker could expect a pension of 13% of average weekly earnings if he survived 11 years past his life expectancy. It really was a safety net for those who lived way past their reasonable working life, and the cost to taxpayers of this system was very minor and quite sustainable.

In what is perhaps the single most important development for humans in thousands of years, dramatic advances in medicine and knowledge for the average person in a first-world society has given us a bonus increase in life expectancy of 25 years in not a lot over a hundred years. So today, the average Aussie male is looking at a life span of close enough to 80 years, and females a few years more. Clearly it would make complete sense to expect to work longer as we lived longer, but much to my amusement, humans being humans, as we live longer we have actually decided to retire earlier. In fact, in the 1990s many spoke of retirement at age 55. Thankfully this wave of optimism has passed, because I have no idea how people would have any hope of leading a reasonable lifestyle for some 30 years in retirement, and at least now we seem to consider 60 a sensible minimum age.

I would not be overly unhappy with age 60 if we planned on spending our couple of decades pottering in the garden as was the case in the past, but that dream has also gone the way of the dinosaurs. Today retirement is about activity. Frankly, it is a much better plan. Travel, eating out, movies, theatre, sport and other cultural and leisure pursuits are now what we plan for in retirement. This is terrific, and ironically, along with the 7.7 million Australians who travelled overseas in 2013, I am typing this on my laptop as I head back from a skiing trip in Italy. However, despite the strong Australian dollar, the simple fact is that this 'new retirement' has a significantly different cost base to tending the roses. What is clear is that it makes sense to plan for two things: a longer life, and a more expensive life.

So how should you and I think about these two huge issues? Let's start by dumping the word 'retirement'. Just as the notion and reality of retirement have changed, the word has become outdated. A better term is 'financial independence'. I like this as a target – it does not commit us to working or not working, but if we achieve it, it gives us more choices about how we live and spend our time. As I approach 60, I don't see myself stopping work, but I will certainly change the amount of work I do and when I do it. These days it's unlikely we'll simply stop working at a particular age. Instead, we will change how we work, when we work and how much we work. This may require new skills and a new attitude from employers, but above all a new attitude from us. Clearly the perfect world is one of true financial independence, where our investment assets generate the inflation-linked income we need for many decades, but this will not be common. For most of us, some work will not only be valuable in maintaining our networks, keeping our minds sharp and bodies active and contributing to our sense of purpose, but also in adding dollars to meet the needs of a potentially long and expensive life.

How much?

Philosophically, longer lives and expensive plans are all very interesting, but we really need to get down to how much money you will need. Once that's established, we can move to how do you do it.

I cannot tell you how much money you will need in retirement. Nor can you, unless you are willing to put in a bit of effort to come up with a realistic description of how you want your life to be and then cost it. It is all very well to look at the perfectly sensible numbers you will see in the media and online about the costs of a basic, comfortable or luxury lifestyle. I keep seeing quotes of around $56 000 a year[1] for a couple who want a 'comfortable lifestyle'. This is a perfectly sensible guide, as are notions of average life expectancy being around 80 years, and that the average family consists of 2.2 children and 13% of a labrador.

Averages are all very interesting, but they are not you. So take a deep breath. If you are in a permanent relationship, grab your partner and a bottle of good red wine and start to jot down your plans at a time when you want to change what you do and how you live. Sixty years is perhaps as good an age as any to start with. I have been married to my wife Vicki for 30 years and we have three children, the youngest just having finished school. I turn 60 in 2015 and Vicki reaches that milestone in 2016, so we think that is as good a time as any to target as a transition point from full-time to more part-time work. We began by assessing our plans from that point on. This included our thoughts

---

1 ASFA Retirement Standard for the June 2013 quarter.

on where we live, how we live, our health, travel, and entertainment needs, our interests in clubs, sport (in particular the cost of my sailing) and allowing the ability to give the kids a financial hand where appropriate. We reviewed and updated our wills, our estate planning and the all-important powers of attorney so that if and when we lose the plot we are prepared for it.

This process enabled us to come up with a number for our annual living costs. This is just critical, because there is no answer to 'how much do I need' if you have no idea of what you want and calculate what that will cost you. Once you have an estimate of how much income you will need at age 60, we can start to do some decent work. As a rule of thumb, whatever income you need at 60, just multiply it by 15 to come up with a starting point for the amount of capital you need. So if you need, say, $50 000 a year, $750 000 becomes your starting capital target.

For all I know, you may need $100 000 a year or more. That is fine, but your capital target will be around $1.5 million. I can hear you thinking, why would I need $1.5 million to give me $100 000 a year? I do know that this only represents a return of a bit over 6% per annum. But there are a couple of problems here. I am assuming that you would want to spread your risk over a variety of asset classes such as cash, fixed interest, property and shares. The other problem is that inflation is running at around 2–3% and if you are going to maintain your spending power in real terms, your capital has to increase along with inflation. We also have other irritations such as tax, which we do need to pay to cover the services we receive from a modern economy, and the inevitable fees that we pay to our accountant or adviser or simply to buy and sell investments.

If, after all that, you can average 3–4% above inflation on your investments, you are doing very well indeed. My 'multiply by 15 at age

60' rule actually assumes that your money will be depleted at around your life expectancy. No doubt, like many, you assume you will get much higher returns – but I am afraid you won't. At the end of the day we will get market returns, less a variety of fees and charges. There are all sorts of high-return, get-rich-quick schemes out there, and they always end in tears. May I remind you that few of us make money out of investing – we make money out of working. We invest our money for hopefully reasonable returns, and we hope not to lose it.

Incidentally, if you want to be financially independent by the age of 55, take your required income at that age and multiply by 17. If age 65 is your target, multiply by 13. Of course this is only a rough rule of thumb – much can go wrong. If you die early, you'll die with money left over. If you live beyond your life expectancy you are likely to run out of funds. If you invest it all in a scam, pyramid scheme, Ponzi scheme or just a dud investment, my rule of thumb will not work. If, like some of my colleagues, you have remarried for the third time at age 55 and have a new baby, a good plan might be to work until you're 90. However, if you estimate you need $100 000 a year and you plan to have $1.5 million in investment assets by the age of 60, things are looking good. But we do need to talk about how you get to your target amount of capital, and we need to start by talking about your home.

The home

Fortunately I have a strong sense of humour. After three decades of giving financial advice I sure need it. One of my favourite themes is along the lines of 'my house is worth a fair bit, what else do I need?' If you do, like so many people, own a home as you reach your sixties, then I am really pleased. But let us not pretend it is part of your investment capital. While owning your home means you don't have to outlay money on rent, your home is in fact an expense. Does your house send you money each month? No, of course not. In fact it costs you to own it – rates, insurance, electricity, repairs and so on.

The average suburban house will cost around $10000 a year to keep in decent condition, with all of the other costs also covered. An apartment may have lower costs, but don't forget your body corporate levies. If we go with my $10000 estimate, then this needs to be put into your annual spending – it is just part of your expenses, and your investment capital needs to produce income to cover the cost of your house or apartment.

If you plan to sell your home, then fair enough – the proceeds become part of your investment income. But where will you live? If you plan to rent, the rent becomes part of your cost base. Downsizing is a legitimate strategy, but please be realistic. Allow for buying and selling costs and take a good look at what you would downsize to. I find that many people move closer to a city in a smaller property, but end up spending most of the sale proceeds of their home. So the question that needs to be answered is whether you will really move properties and add to your capital base.

That I'll leave to you to work out. Hopefully you're further across the notion of planning for financial independence, armed with a plan about what your life will look like, what it will cost a year and your capital needs.

Investing

To determine how you want to invest you first need to have a really firm grip on your cashflow. We make money by working and spending less than we earn. You may get an inheritance or win lotto, but day-to-day living depends upon your work and cashflow. If you need assistance in determining your cashflow, go to the terrific ASIC MoneySmart website and use the online budget planner.

Once you have a sense of your cashflow the next step is to clear any high-interest debts. When these basics are done we can start getting you to your capital target.

Remember that super is not an investment – it is a tax structure. So with surplus income we can really only look at investing it into our business, property, shares or cash and fixed interest. Thank heavens that when I was in my twenties I did not invest in super. I took a much bigger risk and started my business ipac securities. It took all of my very modest capital and I was paid way below market salary for years, but the business prospered. In comparison to super, the returns were vastly higher. But I was much younger and the risk was appropriate for my age. As I outlined in the previous chapter, today super is much more appropriate for me.

I can really only outline the characteristics of investments. How you use them depends upon you, your age, your attitude to risk, and so on.

One of the major areas of interest to investors is shares or property. Over the decades, both have performed well. Personally, as I get older I dilute my risk by going with a mix of shares and commercial, industrial and residential property and fixed interest. Any of these can be acquired by direct investment or via a listed, unlisted or syndicated trust. Each of these can be bought in your name, a company structure, a family trust or a super fund.

This may be sounding a little complicated, but it is not really that hard. There are only a few asset classes we can invest in: property, shares and interest-bearing investments.

Property is a very familiar asset for all Australians. It is very close to our heart, and the dream of home ownership remains as strong today as ever. One of our first big financial decisions is likely to have been to buy a home. Vicki and I did this back in 1983, like so many young couples pretty much within a year of marrying. The fact that it was a small semi-detached home on a busy road facing an industrial estate is merely detail – it was our home.

Every spare dollar we had went into the mortgage and improvements to our home. Like millions of other young couples, this paid off for us. Values increased, we had more children, traded up to a bigger home, and so on. Debt in the form of a mortgage was invaluable, as without it we could not have ever bought a home. Clearly super has nothing to do with this, and nor should it. But it is of little surprise that property values have increased over time. At times they go up, at times they go down, however the fact was then and is now that our population is growing. Add this to a scarcity of land appropriate for housing with modern facilities such as public transport, education, health, leisure and a good coffee shop, and while prices will go up and down, over time it is a pretty simple equation. We have a shortage of supply and high demand. Buy sensibly and over the decades property should do just fine as an investment or as a home.

Shares are also not too hard to understand for a long-term investor. As a short-term punt, you may as well go to the races. But if you, like me, are investing for decades, investments in banks, food sellers such as Woolworths, health-related companies, big miners such as BHP and so on are generally reliable, again due to high local and overseas demand for goods and services. At times shares will fall dramatically, but I'll just ignore that. Prior to the GFC[2] CBA shares were well over $50. They fell to around $24 in the worst of the crisis. However, at the time of writing in 2013 they are around $75. Even better, the bit I spend, the dividends, have been very strong. The only losers here were those who panicked and sold at the low point.

---

2 The global financial crisis ('GFC'), started in August 2007, as a result of a loss of confidence in the value of subprime mortgages in the United States.

Fixed interest is not my favourite, but I do hold some as a nice, secure but low-return investment that I fear will struggle to keep pace with inflation over the long term. Given that various computer models such as 'Death Clock' tell me that statistically I am likely to get pretty close to 90 years of age, I am investing for 30-plus years. I need a growing income stream and growing asset values to keep pace with inflation.

I can hold all of these assets in a super fund, and as you will read in Chapter 7 these days you can borrow in your own DIY fund to buy property. However, one alternative to super that many people use is borrowing to buy an investment property, which we Aussies usually refer to as 'negative gearing'. This is where you borrow pretty much 100% of a property's value and take a tax deduction on your costs of owning the property, which is the interest on your mortgage as well as rates, insurance, agents' fees and so on. Until recently this gearing strategy could not be used inside a super fund, and this change to the legislation has been a big driver in people setting up DIY funds.

Remember: super is not an investment, it is a tax structure inside which you can make investments. Tax is the primary issue. You can put up to $25 000 a year into super from your salary, but do remember to include the compulsory super in the calculation – it is a total maximum annual contribution of $25 000 (though this may be $35 000 for older super members). You can also put in $150 000 a year of your own money, and you can bring it forward three years, meaning you can contribute $450 000 in one year (and nothing in the following two years). The logic here will be tax. Super funds only pay 15% tax on investment income and 10% on capital gains, so putting spare cash into super that you do not need is a good plan as most of us will pay more than 15% tax on investments in our own name outside of super.

I suspect that your wealth creation plans are likely to run along the lines of buying a home and getting the mortgage under control, then perhaps purchasing an investment property and a few shares. The compulsory contributions your employer puts into super for you will build up, and one day you will look at your statement and realise super is turning into real money. You'll get a bit serious and that is why you are reading this.

What type of fund?

So once you realise super is for you, then you need to look at whether you use an industry fund, or a retail fund run by your bank, insurance company or other manager. Whichever way you go, you need to understand the fees and charges, the performance of your fund and the insurance you may have in your fund. Do try to keep your super in just one fund. And if you have no real interest in getting involved in running your own fund, then a DIY fund is probably not for you.

DIY, of course, stands for 'Do It Yourself'. That means you have to get involved, make investment decisions and ensure your fund complies with the legislation. It makes me laugh when I see DIY funds investing with a large fund manager. This is just silly. You pay $5000 or so a year to run and audit your fund and then you pay fees to use a manager that is very likely to have specialist super products that you can invest directly into. Why pay DIY fees and manager fees?

You may also find you get stuck with more than one fund. I am in that situation. I have a DIY fund where I make direct investments, and my employer's fund where my compulsory super goes. Yes, I know I could roll it into my DIY fund, but my employer pays all the manager and administration fees inside my work fund and provides insurance cover, so for now it makes sense for me to have two funds. But when I stop full-time work, I'll roll it all into my DIY fund. And if I ever lose interest in running my own fund, or get a bit past it, I think I will roll it into a managed super fund to remove the hassle. But that's for the future.

So, having looked at the big picture – how much you need, strategies to create it and a quick overview of your super choices – let's get into the main subject matter of this book: DIY super. The next two chapters provide some more background about our Australian super system as a platform for discussion on DIY super. The technical substance is provided by my trusted colleague Peter Crump, a superannuation specialist.

CHAPTER 2

Super choices

There are lots of choices that need to be made about superannuation. We have already looked at how much you need for your retirement. This then leads to the question of how you get there. The journey of 'getting there' is influenced by how much you contribute to super and how you invest the balance along the way.

Let's look at the contributions side first. What contributions do you need to make on a regular basis to achieve your retirement goals? How do you make these contributions and make them in an efficient way?

What types of contributions are there, and how do they work?

The majority of working Australians have some form of superannuation. Those working for an employer have compulsory superannuation contributions paid for them, which are called 'superannuation guarantee' contributions. Those working for themselves are able to make their own contributions.

Our compulsory superannuation system has been in place since 1992 and currently requires that employers make a contribution of at least 9.25% of salary into a superannuation fund that is nominated by

the employee. It is legislated that the level of compulsory superannuation payments will gradually increase from July 2013 from 9.25% of
salary up to 12% of salary from July 2019.

What about your own contributions?

Even if your employer is contributing 12% of your salary into super,
you are likely to need to save even more to give you the retirement lifestyle you are seeking.[1] That said, there are some good tax advantages
that can improve the value of contributions you can make to super
that are definitely worth exploring.

So what options can you consider with your employer? To understand the first of these options requires an understanding of how
'salary sacrifice' works.

Salary sacrifice

When you 'salary sacrifice' you forgo some of your salary in exchange
for taking the payment in an alternative form, such as additional super
contributions. Super contributions are one of the few things that can
be sacrificed without incurring an additional tax called 'fringe benefits tax'. This tax is added to the cost of other items that are paid for
by a salary sacrifice amount, to ensure that the well off are not able
to take advantage of this arrangement. There are only a few tax-effi-
cient opportunities left for salary sacrificing, with super contributions
being the main one, if you can afford to do without the salary in the
meantime.

Let's look at an example of salary sacrifice.

Mary is an employee with an annual salary of $100 000 and

---

1 This conclusion has been made in a series of reports prepared by Rice Warner Actuaries for
the Financial Services Council, which determines the 'retirement savings gap' between what is
required for a reasonable retirement and what is provided by your super and age pension.

her employer makes a super contribution of $10 000 each year. Her employer increases her salary by $10 000 per year and asks Mary if she would like to salary-sacrifice the increase as an ongoing superannuation contribution.

If Mary elects to take the super salary-sacrifice option, the extra $10 000 is paid into a super fund of her choice. Since the contribution is paid by her employer it is subject to 15% contributions tax, which means that the $10 000 super contribution will result in an increase in her super balance of $8500.

When Mary retires and takes her superannuation as a lump sum or pension, according to the super rules, there should be no tax paid on these benefits after she reaches 60 years of age. Mary's salary-sacrificed $10 000 has increased her retirement benefits by $8500 plus the future investment earnings on that amount.

However, if Mary had not elected to salary sacrifice the super but had taken the additional amount as salary – in her hand – she would have paid tax on that amount at the rate of 38.5 cents in the dollar (allowing for the marginal rate of tax of 37% plus 1.5%[2] Medicare levy). This would have left $6150 for Mary to either spend or save. If Mary then contributed that net amount to her super, this would increase her balance by $6150, which compares to the $8500 increase under the salary-sacrifice option.

Assuming that Mary can afford to do without the additional income, using salary sacrifice and superannuation can produce a better outcome over the long term. Why is that the case? It all comes down to a comparison of the effects on her taxation. Money taken as salary-sacrificed super is taxed at 15%, whereas money taken as salary

---

2 At the time of writing, the Medicare levy was 1.5%, and had been announced to increase to 2.0% from 1 July 2014. The advantage of salary sacrificing into super is even better with a higher rate of Medicare levy.

is taxed at the normal marginal rate. If your marginal tax rate is in excess of 15%, salary-sacrificed super is worth looking at.

SUPER TIP

Next time you get a pay rise, look at whether you can salary sacrifice the increase to super. Compare the rate of tax you would pay on that pay rise to the 15% contributions tax you would pay if it went straight into your super. If you're paying more tax if you take that money as cash in hand, and you can afford to live without that pay rise in your hand, then salary sacrificing the pay rise into super can be a good idea.

There are annual superannuation limits or caps, so you need to be aware of these and careful about the amount of contribution your employer is making, as well as any salary-sacrifice contributions. Any super contributions, including salary-sacrifice contributions, that exceed the annual cap incur additional (penalty) tax, which makes them far less tax effective.

For the 2013/2014 financial year, a $25 000 annual contribution limit applies for those under the age of 60, with a $35 000 limit for those over 59. From the start of the 2014/2015 financial year this higher limit of $35 000 will be extended to those over the age of just 49. Any employer contributions above your limit can be refunded to you and taxed at your normal marginal rates, or you can leave them in super and have them taxed at a total rate of 46.5%.

SUPER TIP

Always know what your expected employer and salary-sacrifice super contributions are going to be each financial year, and ensure that they do not exceed the annual limit.

Government co-contributions

As well as tax advantages being available for salary-sacrifice contributions, there is also tax support provided for those who are working and on lower incomes. This support is provided under the federal government's 'co-contribution' arrangements. It works in a pretty simple manner, whereby the government will give you bonus super contributions if you are prepared to make your own personal super contributions – but only if your income is below a certain level. The lower income levels at which the co-contribution subsidy applies are generally too low for super salary sacrifice to work effectively, so the two strategies don't cross over each other.

The co-contribution applies for the first $1000 of personal contributions that you make in a financial year.

The generosity of the co-contribution scheme has been reduced over recent years, and it is now offering a maximum of 50 cents in the dollar subsidy for eligible personal contributions. You will need to look at your total income to determine the actual subsidy that will apply for your personal contributions before you make them.

For the financial year 2013/2014, a maximum co-contribution payment of $500 is paid if your 'income' is less than $33 516. ('Income' generally means 'assessable income' – the income you declare in your personal tax return, plus any employer contributions that are in excess of the compulsory superannuation guarantee amount.)

For the financial year 2013/2014 the co-contribution reduces if your 'income' is between $33 516 and $48 516, with the maximum co-contribution reducing from $500 at the income level of $33 516 to nil at the income level of $48 516. If your income is above $48 516 you are not eligible for the co-contribution.

These co-contribution limits can be indexed each year. It takes the Taxation Office some time to make the co-contribution payment to your super fund, since it is first necessary for them to match the information from your personal tax return against the information provided by your super fund about the contributions that it has received for you. The later you lodge your personal tax return the longer it will take for this matching process to occur, and the greater the delay before your super fund receives the co-contribution.

> **SUPER TIP**
>
> If you are working and can afford to do without $1000 each year, and your 'income' is less than $33 516 (for the financial year 2013/2014), making a personal contribution of $1000 brings an immediate reward of $500 in your super account. In this case that's an overnight 50% return with no risk.

Contributions tax refund

As well as the possibility of this co-contribution subsidy, for low-income earners there is also the potential for a refund of some of the contributions tax that has been deducted from the compulsory (superannuation guarantee) contributions during the year.[3]

If you are working and your 'income' is less than $37 000 (in the financial year 2013/2014), the contributions tax that was taken from your compulsory superannuation guarantee contributions will be returned to your super account up to a maximum refund of $500. In the 2012/2013 year, a person on $37 000 a year received superannuation guarantee contributions of $3330 (being 9% of $37 000), and the 15% contributions tax takes $499.50 from those super contributions. This tax take will be returned to your account only if your income was less than $37 000. If your income is above that level, there is no refund available.

---

3 At the time of writing, the Coalition government had stated its intention to wind back this return of contributions tax to the lower paid.

In both cases, the co-contribution subsidy and the refund of contributions tax, it is not necessary for you to request that these occur; they are automatically paid based on the information in your personal tax return and the superannuation fund's returns.

Spouse contributions

There are other opportunities to make super contributions and to gain a tax advantage, including spouse contributions, which attract a rebate that is based on your income.

If your spouse has assessable income of less than $13 800 (financial year 2013/2014), you are able to make personal contributions to their super account, and claim a 'tax offset' of up to $540.

If your spouse's assessable income is less than $10 800 (financial year 2013/2014), the tax offset is determined as 18% of the first $3000 of contributions that you make for them. If their assessable income is above $10 800, the maximum tax offset reduces to nil at an assessable income of $13 800.

These income levels have not been changed since this special arrangement commenced. Also, the eligibility for these rebates and co-contributions changes on a frequent basis, so you will need to seek advice before making contributions with the intention of gaining a tax advantage.

Personal contributions

After we have used up all of the opportunities for the tax advantages that are afforded to salary-sacrifice contributions, personal contributions with the co-contribution subsidy or spouse rebate, and the refund of contributions tax, what have you got left?

Just plain old personal contributions, which attract neither a tax advantage at the time they are made (that's the bad news) nor any contributions tax within the fund (that's the good news). Each dollar of personal contributions is worth the same dollar within the super fund, and is then fully available to be invested according to your instructions. That said, don't forget that our superannuation system is provided with tax advantages along the way, with investment income being taxed on a concessional basis. Within super, earnings are taxed at a maximum of 15 cents in the dollar, while capital gains are generally taxed at a maximum of 10 cents in the dollar when they are realised.

Additional personal contributions can assist you to reach your retirement target, as these contributions can be invested in the tax-effective superannuation system until retirement. Options on how to invest your super are discussed later in the book.

How do you make contributions?

In the vast majority of cases, contributions are made as electronic transfers to super funds, although some payments might still be made by cheque.

'In-specie' contributions

It is possible for contributions to be made on what is called an 'in-specie' basis, which means that the contribution is not by cash but by an 'in kind' payment of an asset that has a determined value. An example of this is the contribution of a commercial property to a self-managed superannuation fund. Why you would do this, and how, is discussed later in the book.

Even though it is possible for large super funds to receive in-specie contributions as listed shares, for example, very few allow this as it creates significant extra work and cost, and is in demand from a relatively small proportion of members.

How do you take your money out?

There is a range of choices as to how you can take your money out of superannuation. There are two forms of payment: lump sum and pension.

Lump sum

It helps to think of your super account in the same way that you think of your bank account, but with some restrictions that apply (we will talk about these shortly). If you are eligible to take money from your super account, you can do this in the same way that you make a withdrawal from your bank account. This withdrawal is called a 'lump sum' payment.

Just as you need to provide the bank with a completed and signed withdrawal form from, say, your savings account, you will need to provide your super fund with a signed request for the lump sum payment. Some super funds might provide you with online access to your super account, and allow you to make lump sum withdrawals to your personal bank account.

Pension

By 'pension', we mean a regular income payment being made to you from your account balance in the super fund. You can elect to take your payments on a regular basis – such as monthly or quarterly – or you can opt to take a single payment at any time during the year.

To qualify as a 'pension', there are minimum amounts that must be paid to you from your pension account during each year. These minimum drawdown amounts are determined based on a percentage of the balance of the pension account at the start of the financial year, illustrated in Table 2.1.

Table 2.1: Minimum Annual Pension Payments

AGE	MINIMUM % ANNUAL PENSION PAYMENTS
Under 65	4% of your super balance
65–74	5%
75–79	6%
80–84	7%
85–89	9%
90–94	11%
95 or more	14%

In recent years, the government had reduced these minimum percentages to recognise the constraints placed on investments by the global financial crisis.

'Preservation' and 'retirement age'

These minimum pension payments are one of a number of rules that the government has applied in exchange for the tax advantages to encourage us to provide for our own retirement. Full or partial self-provision for retirement will reduce the load on the age-pension purse.

We will investigate some of these rules later in the book, but another relates to when you can elect to take out your super. This restriction is called 'preservation', which means that you are required to keep your money in super (or 'preserve' it) until you meet one of the criteria for being able to access it.

The most extreme of these payment criteria are death or total and permanent disablement, under which circumstances the super balance is needed by the family or the person to support them in their future life.

The majority of super fund members become entitled to receive their balance on attaining 'retirement age', which is currently set at age 65 – the Age Pension age for the majority of Australians.

If you were born after 1 July 1952, you will need to wait a bit longer, as illustrated in Table 2.2.

Table 2.2: Pension Age

DATE OF BIRTH	PENSION AGE	TAKES EFFECT FROM
1 July 1952 to 31 December 1953	65 years and 6 months	1 July 2017
1 January 1954 to 30 June 1955	66 years	1 July 2019
1 July 1955 to 31 December 1956	66 years and 6 months	1 July 2021
1 January 1957 and after	67 years	1 July 2023

Your super can also be accessed earlier if you cease employment after the age of 60 regardless of whether that is a permanent retirement or just temporary. Before age 60, you can access your super if you have attained your 'preservation age' and can confirm that you are permanently retired.

To recognise the increasing need to encourage people to keep their superannuation for longer, the federal government has legislated some time ago for the 'preservation age' to increase from 55 to 60 years of age, depending on your date of birth. This starts to take effect from 1 July 2015, as illustrated in Table 2.3.

Table 2.3: Preservation Ages

DATE OF BIRTH	PRESERVATION AGE
Before 1 July 1960	55
1 July 1960 to 30 June 1961	56
1 July 1961 to 30 June 1962	57
1 July 1962 to 30 June 1963	58
1 July 1963 to 30 June 1964	59
1 July 1964 and after	60

This means that if you were born in 1968, for example, your preservation age will be age 60, unless there are further changes between now and 2028.

'Transition to retirement' pension

Your super is not all totally locked away until you retire. After you have reached your preservation age you can request that some or all of your super balance be made available to you as a 'pension'. This type of pension is called a 'transition to retirement' pension, which means that you can draw against the pension while still working, but you can enjoy some of the pension privileges associated with retirement.

To ensure that you don't blow your super before you have retired, there is an upper limit of 10% of your account balance that can be taken as a pension each financial year until you meet one of the preservation release conditions that were discussed earlier, being:

- turning 65
- leaving employment after 60 years of age
- reaching permanent retirement before turning 60.

All of these rules and restrictions apply across all superannuation funds, including your own super fund. It's important to know about them and to understand them, since they can be very helpful to you when used properly, but need to be complied with to avoid harsh penalties. More of that in later chapters.

How are benefits paid?

Benefits can be paid out of super in cash or in kind (in-specie). As previously discussed, the concept of in-specie transfers or payments is not common in large super funds, since it is a high-cost activity that may be of interest for only a small proportion of members.

However, in your own super fund payment of lump sum benefits (when eligible to do so) on an in-specie basis can provide major advantages. This highlights one of the major differences between being a member of a large fund and having your own super fund.

Let's look at the types of super funds that are out there.

Is there a choice of fund available?

Ever since the start of the compulsory superannuation system there have been restrictions placed on the funds into which these compulsory contributions can be paid. Initially, these funds were specified under industrial awards and then enterprise bargaining agreements (EBAs).

'Choice of Fund' was introduced in 2005, and allowed employees to nominate the super fund into which they wished their employer to direct their compulsory super contributions. There remained industrial and award restrictions under some awards, which specified the funds into which contributions were to be made.

As from 1 July 2013 there is a limited number of funds that can be offered by employers as their 'default' super funds, which are used if an employee does not make an election for the fund into which their compulsory contributions must be paid. Employees retain the choice of super fund that they can use, and they simply need to advise their employer about their preferred fund for that to occur.

There are no restrictions on the direction of super contributions made by the self-employed, who have full flexibility about where they direct their contributions. These decisions are based around convenience and utility.

What types of super funds are there?
'Accumulation' and 'defined benefit' funds

This book doesn't focus on superannuation schemes that are available to government and other public-sector employees, as these operate under more complex conditions and can include what is referred to as 'defined benefit' arrangements.

By far the majority of Australians are members of what are called 'accumulation' funds, where the balance is determined by contributions as well as the fund's underlying investment returns. There is no predetermined final benefit.

The account balance of an accumulation super fund is updated each year by the following additions and subtractions:

	Account balance at the start of the year
Plus	Employer and member contributions
Plus	Rollovers from other superannuation funds
Less	Taxes on contributions and investment earnings
Less	Account expenses
Less	Insurance premiums
Less	Benefit or pension payments (when eligible)
Plus	Investment earnings on the account balance
Gives	Account balance at the end of the year

The two most significant areas where a person can influence the growth of their accumulation account balance over time are the level of contributions made by or on behalf of that person, and the way that the funds are invested.

For the remainder of this book, we will be looking at the accumulation arrangements that apply for most Australians.

Current statistics

The Australian superannuation system is divided into the following types of superannuation funds:

- public sector funds
- corporate (company) funds
- industry funds
- retail funds
- small funds.

Each year, the regulator of these funds, the Australian Prudential Regulation Authority (APRA), publishes statistics about the size and growth of the superannuation system in Australia. Table 2.4 is a snapshot as at 30 June 2013.[4].

Table 2.4: The Size of Superannuation Funds in Australia

	CORPORATE	PUBLIC SECTOR	INDUSTRY	RETAIL	SMALL FUNDS	TOTAL
Number of Funds	108	38	52	127	512 000	512 325
Number of member accounts	500 000	3 300 000	12 000 000	15 000 000	970 000	31 770 000
Assets (billion $)	61.7	256.8	323.2	422.4	507.2	1571.3
Average account balance	$123 000	$78 000	$27 000	$28 000	$523 000	$123 000

4 Source: APRA, Superannuation Quarterly Performance – June 2013. Number of member accounts is estimated.

Number of accounts

The Australian population – from newborns to the very oldest Australians – is around 23 million. There are around 17 million people aged 20 and over, of whom it is estimated that around 12 million would have some form of superannuation account or pension account.

Very interestingly, there were around 32 million accounts as at mid-2013, which means that there are two-and-a-half times as many superannuation accounts as there are members of superannuation funds.

This means that the 'average' Australian superannuation holder has two-and-a-half super accounts. However, in practice, there is a large number of people who have only one super account, which means that there must be some people with three, four or more accounts. If you have more than one super account you are incurring fees for each account, which means that you may be paying more in fees than you need to.

> **SUPER TIP**
>
> Do you receive a member statement from more than one super fund a year? If you do, you have more than one super account and you could be paying two or more sets of fees for your super. Talk to each of the funds about the advantages of consolidating your accounts into one fund to save your costs.

Worse still, if you have moved jobs a number of times you may have had super paid to a number of different funds. Some of those funds may have lost contact with you, or may never have made contact with you. Any super in those funds is passed to the federal government as unclaimed moneys.

SUPER TIP

If you have changed jobs and think that you might have left super behind, have a look to see if you have any unclaimed super by using the ATO's SuperSeeker website.

Size of accounts

Before you get worried about the relatively small size of the assets shown for the public sector funds, it's important to remember that the majority of these funds are 'unfunded' with benefits being paid from consolidated revenue. If you allowed for the public sector unfunded liability, their asset and average account size would be much bigger.

If we adjust the number of accounts in industry funds and retail funds to allow for multiple accounts per person, and assume for the moment that each person has two-and-a-half member accounts, the adjusted average account balances per member are getting up to $70 000.

The higher average account balance for corporate funds (around $120 000) is likely to be a result of the longer period over which these funds have been in place and a more generous level of contribution than just the compulsory rate.

What stands out in the table are the figures relating to small funds. There is in excess of 510 000 of these funds, with an average account balance of over $500 000. These two statistics show the sheer volume of activity in the small-fund area. The value and opportunity from these small funds is explored in later chapters. Small super funds account for almost one-third of the total superannuation assets, and this is growing.

How do the different types of super funds work?
Public sector super funds

Public sector funds are made available only to employees in the federal or state public sector, as well as publicly funded services such as emergency and military services. These funds are often complex and their design is based around a number of features, often related to the length of service and 'seniority' of the individual within the system. As discussed earlier, these funds may be supported out of consolidated government revenue, rather than being funded with real contributions.

If you work in the public sector have a good look at joining these funds if you are eligible to do so, since they are often more generous than those available to the average worker in the non-government sector.

Corporate (company) super funds

Corporate (company) super funds are similar to public sector funds in that they are available exclusively to employees of a particular company. The features of these funds are often the result of years of ongoing negotiation and discussion between company management and employees and their representative unions.

Company funds normally provide benefits that are supported by contributions more generous than the compulsory superannuation guarantee contributions. One of the disadvantages of company funds is that you generally must leave the fund when you stop working with that company.

As shown in Table 2.4, the vast majority of superannuation accounts are in industry and retail super funds. These funds operate in a highly competitive commercial environment, as evidenced by the ongoing advertising in press and television.

Industry super funds

Industry super funds originated in the mid-1980s, prior to the advent of compulsory award-based superannuation. From the outset of the Superannuation Guarantee system in 1992, industry funds were prominent. While these funds started as union-based funds, they have since matured into funds that are evenly supported by employer groups and trade unions, with equal representation across their controlling board or trustees.

Industry funds operate on a 'mutual' basis, where there are no shareholders to whom a share of profits needs to be paid. These funds are presented as being low-cost providers, where there are no margins taken to be paid to agents, advisers or other intermediaries for referring business.

These funds started out to offer a simple 'bulk' superannuation commodity to their members, with the emphasis on low-cost and high-volume offer. Ongoing rationalisation in the industry fund sector has seen already large funds merge with other large funds in their desire to seek scale and maintain their low-cost infrastructure.

Over time, these industry funds have recognised the need to offer a larger range of services and facilities to their members, some of which are offered within the existing cost structure and others as additional cost items.

Insurance through the fund

Most industry funds provide their members with a simple scale of death and TPD ('total and permanent disability') insurance cover, which can be purchased for simple premiums of $1.00 or $1.50 per week for each unit of cover. Some funds provide members with the ability to insure their income under 'income protection' insurance arrangements.

Special insurance concessions are provided to members when they join industry funds on changing jobs and on being eligible to join the fund for the first time. 'Medical-free' insurance cover can be provided within generous limits, which means that a person with an existing (and often unknown) medical condition can obtain insurance cover as a result of participating in a bulk participation arrangement. If that insurance had been available only subject to medical testing, it is possible that cover might not have been offered or might have been offered with higher than normal premiums.

Investment choices

The original investment offerings of industry funds were simple and targeted at the average member, providing relatively few choices. Over time, there has been a gradual addition of further investment options, to ensure that they provide a fuller range of options to their members. For example, some funds include a limited number of listed shares in their investment options, but might impose a limit on the proportion of the overall account that can be invested in one or all of these shares. There may also be restrictions on how often you can buy and sell shares in your super account. You should check these rules before you start this investment.

These changes to the investment offering are examples of industry funds wanting to remain competitive and a viable alternative to the retail super funds and small super funds. They need to keep adding to their services to remain competitive in the superannuation consumer market.

Industry funds often have their own in-house or 'preferred' financial advisers who are available to provide generic advice (at no cost) or personal advice (at cost to the member).

Retail super funds

Retail super funds have been part of the Australian superannuation landscape since the 1960s, but have come a long way since then. These funds are offered to employees as part of a suite of financial services, including superannuation funds, investment funds and life insurance, in a profit-conscious (some might say profit-driven) manner. Invariably these companies have shareholders who expect to receive a return on their investment, and a portion of the profits derived from the activity of the retail super fund goes to these shareholders.

Retail funds are continually developing and evolving their offerings to potential consumers (members), with the intention of providing greater choice, flexibility and options than other retail super funds and industry funds.

Retail funds can be accessed by members of the public directly, without requiring the services of an agent, financial planner or adviser, although the majority of members would have some form of connection with one of these.

The range of investment options offered by retail super funds is often extensive (and exhausting!), with financial advisers being able to assist their clients in selecting one or a number of investment options that is suited to their particular circumstances. It is common for the investment options to include listed shares, generally with restrictions, such as only including shares in Australia's largest 300 companies (the 'ASX300').

Members of retail super funds can select their required insurance cover for death, total and permanent disability or income protection, but the insurance cover is normally subject to some form of medical assessment. The higher the level of cover, the greater the detail of the medical, from simple health-related questions at the lower end to detailed health assessment procedures for very high cover.

Both retail and industry funds provide their members with the ability to have super balances in either accumulation or pension state. For both types of funds, detailed forms are required to be completed to request to join the fund and to make changes (such as from accumulation to pension) or to add insurance.

The trustee

All super funds (public sector, company, industry and retail) have a trustee that takes responsibility to ensure that all of the super legislation and rules are met. The trustee makes decisions about who provides the administration, insurance and investment services to the fund, and is responsible for supervising these service providers and to ensure that they meet any service standards. Members can select from the menu of insurance and investment choices offered to them by the trustee, and cannot add to these choices. If the member can't find what they want, they need to go to another fund that can meet that need. Which brings us to the so-called small funds.

Small funds

'Small funds' is the generic description given to super funds that have fewer than five members. Within the small-funds group are two types, the first being where a professional (commercial) company provides trustee services. These funds are called 'small APRA funds' or SAFs, since they are supervised and regulated by APRA (the Australian Prudential Regulation Authority). APRA is responsible for regulating all funds of more than four members as well as small funds that have a professional trustee company.

The SAF trustee has all of the responsibilities of a trustee under superannuation legislation, but is more open to accommodating (commercially acceptable) tailored investment options, such as property investment. These investment arrangements are supported within tight business constraints, as the trustee company bears the risk of non-compliance and incorrect record-keeping.

The other type of small fund, and these are in the majority, are 'self-managed superannuation funds' or SMSFs, which is the label given to funds where the members and the trustees are one and the same. In these funds, the trustees are generally able to accommodate the requests or expectations of the members (as, after all, they are the same people), so long as they are within the law. That is why these funds are often called 'Do It Yourself' or DIY funds.

The investments you can have in SMSFs are much broader than can be accommodated in more constrained environments where there is a commercial arms-length trustee accountable for the conduct of the fund. As will be discussed in later chapters, in your own super fund you can undertake much more active strategies and actions, with minimal paperwork and red tape, so long as they are within the law.

There are costs involved in running your own super fund, and you need to choose how much you want to do yourself and how much you would like to do with assistance from experts. Costs of running a DIY super fund will be discussed in later chapters.

Starting out

Having your own super fund involves set-up costs and ongoing costs, some of which are fixed regardless of the size of your balances.

When you are first starting out, having a simple super fund arrangement with low costs is the best option. That is why most people start with an industry fund or retail fund before they move to their own super fund.

> **SUPER TIP**
> Start out simple and move to your own super fund when you have enough to make it work for you.

There are a large number of highly competitive super-fund arrangements available from which to choose. Despite that, many

Australians have already set up their own super fund, and more are following them each day. So many are voting with their feet, tired of paying managers to lose their money, tired of fees, and wanting to do better with their own super fund. DIY funds are on the rise.

CHAPTER 3

Do-it-yourself super

So what's so special about DIY funds that 970 000 Australians have chosen to have one? If you don't have your own super fund, are you missing out on something? What do you need to think about before venturing down the path of establishing and controlling your own super fund?

Australians are well known for wanting to 'have a go', and the idea of running your own super fund taps into that part of our psyche. You don't need to be wealthy to have your own super fund, but it helps to have a good understanding of what superannuation is all about and the rules you need to meet to stay within the law and out of jail.

Globally we are not alone in our enthusiasm for DIY funds. People in the United States have had their '401(k)' funds since the 1980s. Here in Australia, we have a superannuation system that is regarded as being one of the world leaders in enabling individuals to save for their retirement.

This history of DIY funds in Australia provides a backdrop to some of the special arrangements in place today – and is a good place to start in reviewing the reasons why you might want to set up your own super fund.

History of DIY funds in Australia

Small super funds have been around for many years, but 1987 marked the start of a new era for the regulation of super funds in Australia, with the first attempt to specifically legislate how super funds could operate. From that time, information has been collected about the number of super funds in place. At that time, DIY funds weren't popular. The major milestones in the growth of DIY funds were 1994, 1999 and 2006, and the growth in popularity of DIY funds at, or shortly after, these years is illustrated in Figure 3.1, which sets out the number of self-managed superannuation funds from 1987 to 2013.

Figure 3.1: Growth of DIY super funds in Australia

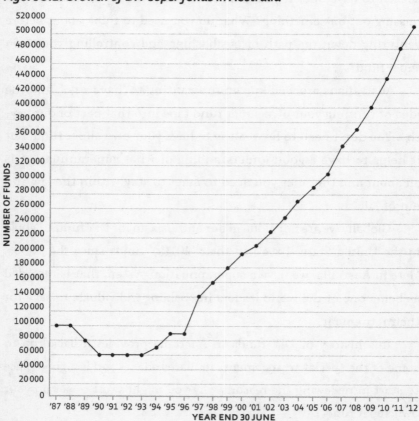

Superannuation funds in Australia are governed by the Superannuation Industry (Supervision) Act, which explains how they must be operated and maintained. The 'SIS Act', as it is often called, was put into place in 1994 after a major review and rewrite of the various pieces of legislation that applied to superannuation funds at that time.

Prior to the SIS Act, the laws governing how superannuation worked and the concessions that applied to it were spread across a number of pieces of legislation, which made it very hard for the average person to obtain reliable information about the rules governing superannuation. This major rewrite made it easier to see what was expected in setting up and managing your own super fund. The 1994 changes opened the door for the establishment of small funds.

This situation was made even more inviting in 1999, when modifications were made to create much of what is still in place today for the regulation of self-managed superannuation funds.

Even the name that was given to small funds made them more inviting. Prior to 1999, small funds were called 'excluded funds', which made them sound uninviting and like some form of exception. The term 'excluded' was used to confirm that these small funds were excluded from a large number of the regulations that applied to the larger funds. At that time the majority of these 'excluded' funds had been established by the self-employed and small-business operators to manage their own superannuation. Under modifications to the SIS Act in 1999, small funds were renamed 'self-managed superannuation funds' (or SMSFs). This much friendlier label continues to be used today. The legislative 'exceptions' that apply to small funds also continue to this day.

The latest major legislative changes affecting superannuation were implemented on 1 July 2007, under the 'Simpler Super' (subsequently renamed 'Better Super') system introduced by the then federal treasurer, Peter Costello. These changes were announced well over a year prior to their implementation, in the May 2006 federal budget, and the next 13 months saw more major growth in the number of SMSFs that were established to take advantage of the transitional measures in place at the time.

> **SUPER TIP**
>
> If you have your own super fund or are thinking about having your own super fund, take 15 minutes to have a look online at the main issues that are covered under the *Superannuation Industry (Supervision) Act* and the *Superannuation Industry (Supervision) Regulations*.

Conditions and privileges

It's important to remember that all superannuation funds must meet basic rules under the legislation, whether they are small funds or large funds. For example, these rules include restrictions on:

- when a fund can accept contributions from a member
- when a fund can make benefit payments to a member
- the amount of pension that can be paid to members.

Privileges are granted to all types of super funds in exchange for meeting these rules, and special taxation concessions are made available to super funds, with a lower rate of tax applying to:

- investment income (taxed at 15%)
- realised capital gains (taxed at 15% on two-thirds of the realised gain for assets sold after being held for more than 12 months, and 15% on the full capital gain if the asset is held for less than 12 months)
- investment income and realised gains for assets supporting pensions (no tax)

- deductible contributions (taxed at 15%) (see Chapter 9, 'Super Strategies').

DIY funds are regulated differently

To better understand why you should consider having your own super fund, let's have a look at why small funds have extra laws that apply to them compared to their larger counterparts – which is why it's worth considering establishing your own super fund.

The larger superannuation funds are supervised by the Australian Prudential Regulation Authority (APRA), which is also responsible for the supervision of the Australian banking and financial system and insurance companies. The activities of APRA are generally funded by levies against the institutions that it supervises.

Table 2.4 in Chapter 2 showed that there were only 287 corporate, industry and retail superannuation funds in total, with total assets of over $800 billion at 30 June 2013. This amounts to an average of $2.8 billion for each fund supervised by APRA.

This is a relatively small number of funds to be supervised, but represents the potential for a very large financial risk to the superannuation of average Australians if these funds are not closely supervised and managed under the supervision of the regulator. These larger funds are therefore subjected to 'prudential' regulation under the legislation.

Trustees of these funds are required to provide regular reports to APRA, and to have comprehensive business plans approved by APRA. This is part of a complex supervisory regime that is based around receiving, analysing and acting on fund information provided to APRA. This is no different to running a large company accountable to shareholders, who expect a prudently run business that performs in accordance with its stated business plan and objectives.

This is a very resource-intensive method of supervision, but one that is able to be applied to the small number of larger superannuation funds. This level of intense reporting and close supervision would be oppressive for small super funds, and you could not survive as a small fund under this arrangement. Fortunately for all of us, the way that small funds are managed under the law is by means of 'compliance-based' regulation.

'Compliance-based' regulation for small funds

By 'compliance-based', we mean that small funds are required to essentially self-regulate their behaviour according to the law, and this behaviour is assessed at the end of each financial year as part of the fund's financial reporting and tax-return lodgement. These annual returns are required to be independently audited, together with the activities of the fund during the year.

If the fund has been operated in accordance with the legal requirements, the audited annual return will confirm this. However if there are activities or behaviours that are not in accordance with the law, these are reported to the regulator.

Small funds are regulated by the Australian Taxation Office (ATO), which is responsible for the supervision and integrity of the SMSF portion of the superannuation industry. It's initially a bit of a shock to consider that the ATO (which most people associate with being a tax collector) is responsible as a supervisor, but it makes sense when you consider why this is the case.

The ATO is well equipped to collect a lot of information from many sources, which is what it does with your personal tax returns and company tax return each financial year. That is why the ATO became the regulator of the SMSF sector from 1999 onwards. Even at that time, however, there could not have been an expectation that the number of funds under its supervision would balloon from 200 000 to 500 000.

As the SMSF regulator, the ATO works on 'exception' reporting, being interested only in those funds that self-report they are not meeting specific requirements under the law. Remember that each SMSF is independently audited at the end of each year, so it should not be possible to escape detection for non-compliance with the law. Based on the audited information provided to it at the end of each financial year, the ATO reviews the funds that are reported as not meeting all of the requirements and also selects a small sample of random funds for its own audit and review.

The ATO selects around 1% of funds for these random audits, but they are not totally random after all. The majority of these ATO audits are selected based on information included in the annual returns that suggests that the fund could be in a 'higher-risk' group of not meeting the rules. Funds in this higher-risk group would include those with loans to related parties or borrowings or direct property investments. Previous experience has given the ATO an instinct that these are likely to be areas that have potential for problems or misadventure.

It's a bit like driving a 'hotted-up' red sports car – it's important that you keep the car fully compliant with the road rules as it is inevitably going to attract police attention. So make sure that if you have a 'hotted-up' super fund you don't have anything to hide if the ATO decides to audit the fund.

It's worth remembering that an audit by the ATO is not a bad thing if you have met all of the legal requirements and are running your fund in the right way and for the right reasons.

The ATO uses the independent auditors as its 'foot soldiers', relying on them to identify actual or potential problems with a fund's compliance and then to report that to the tax man. This level of scrutiny means that you should always run your fund within the law, as you are likely to get caught out if you don't. As will be discussed later, there are financial and other penalties that can be applied if you don't meet the rules.

This regulation by the ATO is not provided without cost, unlike the personal and business taxation system, which is a government-provided service. A formal levy is applied against all small super funds to ensure that the supervisory services of the ATO are funded by these funds. For the 2013/2014 year, the ATO's supervisory levy was $259 per fund, and this is expected to increase over time. This is the only compulsory fixed cost that you incur if you have your own super fund. All of the other costs can be negotiated, reduced or avoided by taking services in house (with the exception of the audit of the fund).

For 500 000 SMSFs, this means that the ATO has over $100 million to spend on supervising and monitoring them. That's a lot of money to spend on running this part of the superannuation system, which is all about protecting the special concessions that the government provides to us through our own super funds.

Greater opportunity but greater regulation

Don't think that self-managed super funds are subject to less legislation or fewer regulations, as there are more sections of the legislation that affect small funds than affect the larger funds. As we have discussed, the main difference for small funds is the way they are monitored and regulated by the ATO. Since the trustees and members are the same, the types of activity that can be undertaken in small super funds are significantly more flexible and based around the specific needs or wants of the members themselves.

Having a small fund is a bit like having a speedboat rather than being a passenger on a large cruise liner. Both types of craft are boats that transport passengers on water. The speedboat is more nimble and can navigate small passages and turn quickly to take its occupants where they want to go. Having chosen and embarked on a large cruise liner, the passengers are able to relax and enjoy the ride and select from the range of activities that are offered to them, while the captain and crew take responsibility for sailing the boat on the agreed voyage. The cruise liner is unable to change its course quickly, even if a few passengers would like to seek alternative destinations.

So what are some of the reasons why we prefer a speedboat (our own super fund) rather than a passage on a cruise liner (retail or industry funds)?

Reasons for setting up your own super fund

Popular reasons for setting up your own super fund include:

- selecting investments that are not available in industry or retail funds
- using super to provide support to your business
- undertaking super strategies that are not readily supported by industry or retail funds
- wanting to do your own thing and manage it yourself.

Let's quickly look at each of these.

Getting access to investments

Retail and industry super funds can provide a lot of opportunities for a lot of people, and the number of people using these funds shows that they provide a popular option for the majority of Australians. There's nothing like healthy competition to bring about product initiatives and options, which can only benefit the members.

But it's important to remember that these funds need to be run in an economic manner, meeting the needs of most of their members as efficiently as possible. As a result, they cannot offer investment options that will meet the needs of all people.

Since these funds are prudentially managed and regulated, they will not offer investments that are highly personalised or subject to higher degrees of risk, such as individual properties or geared investment arrangements, where there is a commercial risk to be considered.

In your own super fund, there is a much broader range of investment opportunities from which you can select, subject only to the limitations imposed by the law, which is why your fund can't lend money to yourself.

The types of investments that you can undertake are discussed later in the book.

SUPER TIP

If you are a member of a retail fund or industry super fund, have a look at the investment menu to see the types of investments available to you. Is there something missing into which you would like to legally invest your super money? If so, it could be time to look more closely at the opportunities provided by having your own super fund.

Using super to support your business

Before you get all excited about using your super to prop up your business, this is one area where there are special rules about what you can and can't do when dealing with your own or a family member's business through your own super fund.

We are continually reminded by the regulator that the purpose of superannuation is to provide for our retirement, and this 'sole purpose test' is the cornerstone of what superannuation is meant to be about.

Using your own super in a way that provides assistance or support to your business can only be undertaken if there is a clear connection with earning investment returns, without unreasonably increasing the risk of losing money if the business does not succeed.

If you've got money in super and your business needs to move to new premises, having your super fund buy the new premises and lease them back to your business provides an opportunity to keep money within the family.

Having your business leasing the property from your super fund means that the business pays the fund the lease payments (at market rates), which are tax deductible to the business and this income is taxed in the super fund at 15% (or lower if some of the members are drawing pensions from the fund). As the business grows over time and there is a need to move to new premises, you can keep the property as an ongoing investment of your fund or you can sell it and pick out a new property.

Chapter 9 covers some of the opportunities you can explore through your own super fund to invest in business property or even business equipment. We'll also have a look at using borrowing to enhance the value from investments, which can provide a 'win–win' opportunity for you, your business and your super fund.

Special strategies in small funds

You will hear a lot of talk about 'strategies' around superannuation, and there is more to super than just investing money. These strategies are about how you can improve your personal tax outcomes or your family's tax outcomes today and in the future – of course within the law.

Tax can interfere with the efficient growth and distribution of wealth through superannuation. So it's important to find out what these strategies are and how you can use them to your benefit. These strategies can be knocked around with changes to legislation or government policy, so it's important to talk with your adviser or accountant before considering using them. The more popular strategies are discussed in Chapter 9.

Doing your own thing and doing it yourself

Our current society is very much about enabling people to do more things for themselves. The explosion of retail hardware stores has meant that the home handyperson is encouraged to undertake some of the less technical home-maintenance activities themselves. The results might not be as polished as a professional might have achieved, and it's not always about doing it cheaper but more about having the satisfaction of having been able to do it yourself.

Running your own investments and making your own decisions about what investments to buy and sell can be a strong motivator to have your own super fund. Just like the home handyperson, who might not know a lot about the activity at hand, help can be sought from professional experts.

Of course, running your own super fund is not quite the same as doing small maintenance jobs around the house – it's more like a major renovation project. It's not for everyone, and some people might undertake it and realise part way through that it is too much for them. On the other hand, there are people who find that they enjoy the challenge so much they get hooked.

Whatever you do, don't let running your own super fund end up running your life. You've worked hard throughout your working life to earn enough for a comfortable and active retirement, so don't mess that up by getting bogged down with the daily grind of your own super fund. You'll work that out as you go, but make sure you ask your partner or spouse or children if they think that you are spending too much time or worrying too much about your super fund. Their opinion is important.

Why the growth in small funds?

There has been a big growth in small funds in recent years – and indeed, you may be part of that. There are some good reasons why this has happened, and it's all to do with investment and how you can carry it out within super.

For instance, late in 2007, the law was changed to allow super funds to borrow to invest. Up until then, borrowing in superannuation funds was permitted only in very restrictive and short-term circumstances, and geared investment was only undertaken outside super. The change of the law resulted in a flurry of activity as the ability to borrow to invest in super was actively and widely promoted. It's not surprising that the number of funds grew from 350 000 in 2007 to 500 000 in 2013.

When investment markets have an extended bad patch and returns are low for a longer period of time, people become frustrated at the losses or low returns that they see the experts making with their own super and believe they can do better. That often turns out to be the case, not because the person is a better investor than the experts, but as a result of a major change in the approach to investing in the current market conditions.

For example, at the start of the global financial crisis (GFC), taking your money out of shares and putting it into term deposits would have produced a better return than leaving the balance in shares, which continued to decline in value.

There is no question that making your own investment decisions enables you to tailor your investments to more closely suit your attitudes to risk and rewards. How you will perform as an investment manager compared to the professionals can only be fairly determined over time, preferably over an extended period during which investment markets move up and down over the full economic cycle.

The other reason why we have seen an explosion in the number of small funds is the expanded financial awareness that the general community has. While the GFC has been a negative throughout the economy, it has sharpened our focus on investing, risk and alternative investments.

Our understanding of investing in shares first took off in the late 1990s, with the listing of Telstra and the demutualisation of the large life insurance companies, such as AMP and National Mutual (AXA). This brought share ownership out of institutions and into the hands of the person in the street. Ever since then, there has been a growth in understanding of share investing, of profits made by large institutions and of the global economy.

It's no wonder that people want to take control of their own super investments when they have participated in this expansion of information and knowledge over such a short period of time. Their super is probably the largest pot of money that they can invest, outside the family home.

So if everyone seems to be doing it, or talking about doing it, is DIY super for you?

CHAPTER 4

Is DIY super for you?

So, you're contemplating setting up your own super fund? What do you need to think about before going down that path?

Start by looking at some reasons why DIY super might not be right for you. To have your own super fund, you also need to be the person that is legally responsible for the fund, which is the 'trustee' of the fund. In fact, each member of the fund must be a trustee of the fund, so let's look at why you may not be able to be a trustee.

Those who can't be a trustee of their own super fund are known as a 'disqualified person'. Put simply, a disqualified person is someone who:

- has been convicted of an offence relating to dishonest conduct
- is an undischarged bankrupt
- has been penalised for breaching one of the major superannuation rules
- has been disqualified by the regulator.

The first two categories apply to first-time trustees and are also the issues that disqualify most people, as there is no time limit on the conviction for a dishonesty offence. This conviction might have occurred when you were much younger, but it still sticks when you want to be a trustee of your own super fund.

If you are planning on being the trustee of your own super fund it's important to know whether you may not meet these criteria, since you need to make a declaration to the ATO at the time of establishing the fund that all trustees are not disqualified persons. It's an offence to make an incorrect declaration.

Some activities are exclusive to self-managed super funds

If you are thinking of investing in a property or a specific type of investment that you can't have in retail or industry super funds, you may be able to hold these in your own super fund. If you want to use borrowed funds you can only do so in your own super fund.

So if property or borrowing is on your agenda for superannuation, your own super fund is the only way to go.

But what if you are not interested in property or borrowing within your super? Is DIY super still for you?

What types of people have a self-managed super fund?

Small funds are set up by people from all backgrounds, not just professionals or white-collar workers. There are some common personality characteristics among those who set up their own super funds.

People who set up their own super fund are often interested in maintaining greater control over their superannuation, as well as their personal finances. This control could relate to just the investment of the assets within their super fund, or could also extend to control over the daily (administrative) activity of the fund.

Those who are interested in taking control of their super are more likely to be interested and engaged in their super. In larger superannuation funds (industry funds and retail super funds) around 40%

of the assets are invested in the fund's default investment strategy (usually a 'balanced' type fund invested in a diversity of growth- and income-producing assets), which suggests that there is a low engagement among members of these funds. However, in small super funds, there is 100% engagement in the investment process.

Recent surveys across the general population suggest a high degree of 'financial illiteracy' when it comes to superannuation, with over 70% of people indicating that they do not understand how their super is invested. These people are unlikely to be interested in running their own super fund.

People with their own super funds have a sense of flexibility and influence, that they are in a better position to respond to changes in the environment or investment market, or can position themselves in anticipation of these changes. Surveys of retail, industry and DIY fund members continually show a higher satisfaction rating from members of DIY funds, which is not surprising as these members are engaged and interested in their super.

However DIY super's appeal is not restricted only to the 'controllers', as there are other personality types that are interested in running their own super fund. The 'coach seekers' are interested in having a degree of control over their funds, but will seek relationships with advisers who can work to assist them without looking to take over control. Coach seekers seek out mentors who can provide information to help them to make their decisions. The trustee will work with an adviser, but it needs to be on the trustee's terms. There is always a desire by the 'coach seeker' trustee to maintain control and have a say about how their retirement savings are invested.

The controllers and coach seekers are at the top end of the independence scale.

Table 4.1: Different Approaches to Self-managed Super Funds

INDEPENDENT	Controllers	'I'm interested in it and I like doing it myself'
	Coach seekers	'I'd rather do things myself but I am looking for help'
DEPENDENT		'I'd rather do things myself but I need information to support me'
	Delegators	'I'd rather someone else do it for me'

Delegators like the special features of having their own super fund, but seek support to provide them with the comfort that their fund is being taken care of and meets all of the legal requirements. Delegators are keen to have a sense of participation in running their own fund, but want independent validation that they are doing the right things.

SUPER TIP

Think about which of these types most matches your personality and then think about how this affects your decision to have your own super fund. What level of external support or help will you want to run your fund?

What type of trustee – personal or company?

Once you have cleared the first hurdle of being 'qualified' you can go on to make the first important decision about your own super fund. You need to decide what type of trustee you want your fund to have – personal trustees or a company as trustee.

More than 70% of small super funds in Australia have personal trustees, but 90% of new funds that are established have personal trustees. This is because it's much easier and faster to set up a small super fund with personal (or individual) trustees, as the decision to set up the new fund can be made and then followed through on the same day by the completion and lodgement of all of the documents necessary to start the fund. It's also cheaper to have personal trustees, as there are no additional costs for that.

So why is it that experts suggest that it's better to use a company as the trustee?

Setting up a new company takes a few days from completion of the forms to receiving confirmation from the Australian Securities and Investment Commission (ASIC), which is the regulator for companies in Australia. The set-up costs are around $600 upwards, and the company has annual costs of regulation of around $50.

One of the main attractions for having a company as a trustee is the convenience it brings with regard to ownership of assets and future changes to trustees and members. With a company as a trustee of your fund, each member of the fund must also be a director of the trustee. This means that each time a new member comes into the fund or a member leaves the fund, it is necessary to change the directors of the company. The assets of the fund continue to be owned in the name of the company, even though there have been changes to the directors.

This contrasts with what happens with changes in members when you have personal trustees, since the ownership of each asset must be changed to reflect any change in trustees. The trustees are acting collectively when they own assets as individual trustees of the fund, and it is important that this collective ownership is properly reflected for each of your super fund's assets at all times.

Another attraction of the company as trustee is that it is possible to have a company with a single director, if you are the only member in your fund. However, if you have personal trustees, it is not possible to have only one personal trustee, as you are required under the law to have two personal trustees when you are the only member of the fund. This means that you must involve another person as a trustee, and share the responsibility of decisions affecting your own super fund.

The third main attraction of having a company as a trustee is that the company acts as a legal barrier between you as a member of the fund and any legal action that may be taken against the trustee of the fund.

So what this all means is that if you are in a hurry to set up your fund, personal trustees are the way to go, but if you are not in a rush and don't mind the additional set-up cost, using a company as trustee can give you greater peace of mind and less hassle later on.

When you set up your fund, you will need to provide information to the ATO, as the regulator of small funds, which will enable it to quickly review the initial trustees and company. The ATO is not obliged to approve the establishment of the new fund and can either query the information or decline the new fund if the trustees include a person who is disqualified or has a poor history with the ATO, such as persistent late lodgement or non-existent personal tax or business tax lodgement and payment.

It's only after the ATO has confirmed that it will allow the new fund to proceed that it publicly confirms the status of the fund on its Fund Lookup website. This site allows members of the public to search for any small fund that is in place.

SUPER TIP

If you have your own super fund, search for it online at Super Fund Lookup to see what information is available to the public about your fund. The information is not enough to personally identify you, but is enough to confirm the fund's genuine existence.

At the time of starting your fund, you will also need to read and sign the Trustee Declaration, which confirms that the new trustees are aware of their responsibilities and duties as well as the penalties that can be applied by the regulator for non-compliance with the law.

SUPER TIP

Are you aware of what you have signed when you started your own super fund? Have another look at the self-managed super fund trustee declaration on the ATO's website. Make sure that you understand what it is talking about. If you don't, ask your trusted adviser to explain.

What services must be delegated?
Trust deed

The trust deed for the fund is a legal document that sets out the rules under which the fund must be operated. It personalises the rules so that they are specific to the fund you have, but these rules cannot be in conflict with the requirements of the superannuation legislation.

Since this is a legal document, a suitably qualified legal practitioner must prepare it for your fund. There are many providers, ranging from online providers to personalised legal advisory services. The trust deed will have a number of supporting documents that relate to it, which need to be used in conjunction with that trust deed.

While cost is something to consider when obtaining a trust deed for your fund, you should remember that this legal document will govern what you can and can't do with your super. The larger your pot of super money or the more complex the strategies you are considering undertaking, the greater the need for a good-quality and tailored trust deed document. If you're not a super expert, make sure your trust deed is provided by someone who is suitably qualified.

It's just like having a will prepared. There are simple will kits that can be purchased over the counter that have very simple provisions and that, when properly completed and executed, can serve the purpose quite effectively. However, for more complex estate arrangements, seeking the input of a professional can ensure there will be no surprises or problems at the time the will needs to be implemented. Unlike a will, however, a trust deed is used on a continuous and ongoing basis, which can affect you while you are still alive. Proceed with care here.

Audit

As we have previously discussed, the small-fund segment of the superannuation industry is governed by compliance-based regulation, and one of the cornerstones of this process is the independent audit of the fund's activities and financial reporting at the end of each financial year. The auditor must be independent of the members of the fund, so you can't have a family member audit your fund and you certainly can't audit your own super fund. Hopefully, the reasons for this are fairly clear: that the audit is intended to be an independent verification that the fund has met the rules.

How you select an auditor is very much up to you. If you have a relationship with an adviser, you could ask them to recommend some potential auditors, or your personal tax adviser could be a useful referral source.

Auditors are governed by their own professional and ethical codes, and are required to raise issues of concern with both the trustees and the regulator, so they are in a difficult position of being an arms-length provider who is really working as the eyes of the regulator. Don't expect any special favours from auditors – if they find a misdemeanour (deliberate or accidental) they are required to report it.

Bank account

You will need to establish and maintain some form of bank account for your fund, which will receive contributions, tax refunds, share dividends and other income, and which will pay out benefits, pensions, fees, taxes and other outgoings. You will need to select a bank account that is appropriate for your needs, just like you would when setting up a personal bank account.

Issues that you will need to think about when selecting a bank account for your super fund include:

- fees
- availability of cheque or online payment facilities
- rate of interest
- accessibility to information (online or paper)
- ATM access (for funds paying pensions).

It's okay to use a bank account for your super fund that is with the same bank you use for personal or business banking, as long as you keep the accounts separate.

As with opening a bank account, your bank will need to confirm that you are appropriately identified and that appropriate anti-money laundering checks are met. So don't be worried when you are opening your fund's bank account that you are asked for a copy of documents that verify the existence and bona fides of the fund and you personally.

The right balance between doing it yourself and seeking assistance

Remember that you remain responsible for your own super fund at all times. You can seek professional assistance and advice to run different aspects of your fund, but you can't afford to sit back and assume that it's all working well. It's your fund, so use it wisely.

Controllers are more sensitive to the fees they pay for the services they seek to support them and their fund. Coach seekers are more likely to seek out a wider range of support and to use that support on an ongoing basis. Delegators will look for support for most of the fund's activities.

In an effective support relationship, advisers can assist you with financial literacy and confidence, which will improve your understanding of the options available to you. While you could get this type of advice from the internet, it's what you don't know about these issues that will be your greatest disadvantage. If you don't know what to look for, you won't know what you are missing out on and you won't know how to apply it in practice.

SUPER TIP

The internet can be a valuable tool for researching ideas and information on super. However, be wary of the source as any actions you take based on information you have accessed online are your own responsibility. If you don't fully understand something, it pays to get formal advice. The ATO website is a good source of information on super, and provides much to consider.

With the exception of the services that must be delegated (trust deed, audit and bank account), you can determine the level at which you would like to engage with providers of the other services. These other services include:

- member record-keeping
- investment record-keeping
- preparation of financial accounts at the end of the financial year
- liaising with the auditor about fund records and information
- preparation and lodgement of the annual tax return
- strategic advice about the management of member accounts and pension accounts

- advice about selecting and managing the investments of the fund according to your strategy and needs
- ensuring compliance with minimum and maximum pension requirements
- ensuring compliance with other legislative requirements, such as those relating to new members or exiting members.

It's important you are comfortable with the competence and skill of any professional service provider you engage to provide support to you in managing your own super fund. How much you use these external services will depend on how much you want to go it alone and how much you want to be supported. Funds that are quite simple in their approach to contributions and investments may not need as much support and guidance as those that are more complex.

It does not do any harm to spend some time researching the various types of service providers that practise in the SMSF area, and to discuss with them what they claim they can do for you and your fund. While there is no 'try before you buy', make sure that you are not locked into a long-term or fixed-contract period with your advisers.

If you don't think that you are getting value from them, tell them and ask them to tell you what they can do for you. If you're still not happy that you are getting value, you can leave them and return to working on your own or look at alternative providers.

Ask your friends or business colleagues who they use and what they have experienced – this is a safer way of determining who might be a good match for you.

Remember it's your time that you are spending on your own super fund and it's your choice as to how much of your time you want to spend. Be careful, though, not to let your super fund become your employment in retirement. You have worked hard to live a comfortable life in retirement, so don't forget to enjoy it! A reminder that if you find that your super fund is stressing you out, it's time to look at what you might need to change. Sharing the responsibility and involving others is one way to reduce stress.

Going it alone, or involving others in your fund

So far, we have spoken about your own super fund as if you were the only member of the fund. One of the early considerations is whether you want to involve other people in your fund – for example, your spouse, business partner or children. Remember it's important to check that any additional members will not fall foul of the 'disqualified persons' requirements.

Your spouse

Why would you want to involve your spouse in your own super fund? It's probably better to think about it the other way and consider why you wouldn't want to involve your spouse, as that's a bit safer for domestic harmony. Only a quarter of SMSFs have one member, with the majority (two-thirds) having two members. Funds with three or four members make up the balance, representing less than 10% of all small funds.

Involving your spouse in your fund makes the fund a 'family' superannuation fund, which starts to create a sense of family wealth and of longer-term planning around this wealth. Being able to share the responsibility and ideas with your spouse can make running your own super fund a lot easier. Is your spouse interested in superannuation or investing? Don't be worried if they are not, because they will still be a great support to you even though they might not be as intensively involved as you are.

Under super law your spouse is able to 'inherit' your super balance in the event of your death without having to take it out of the fund. This means that the investments you have selected as being of value to you and your family can survive you and can be continued on by your spouse. Involving your spouse in the family super fund, even at a lighter level than you, will ensure they develop some understanding about how it works and will be able to continue it after your death.

While you might be more of a controller personality, your spouse might be more of a coach seeker or delegator, which means that you need to discuss with them what options they will have to continue the fund with some degree of professional support.

Don't feel concerned about talking about what happens with your super fund after your death, because that's one of the important features of our super system, that it allows for super to be kept going by your spouse after your death. This means that you can take a much longer-term approach to how you are investing, since you are investing for two people's life expectancies rather than just one.

It's not only the collective decision-making and support that your spouse brings, but also extra super dollars into the fund. Now you've got not only your own super money but also your spouse's in the fund, which will help you to build up a critical mass of investment funds and give you scale over which to spread the costs of running the fund. If you would like to use your super to buy a property, having more money in super makes this easier, which is why having two members can be helpful.

We'll talk a bit later about what happens in your super fund if you and your spouse are no longer seeing eye to eye. That can make being in the same super fund a bit tricky.

Your business partner

When you're in business together, you spend a lot of time with your business partner – possibly more than with your spouse – so it's very important to select the right person with whom to go into business. If the business is leasing a property for its business premises, it's quite common for that property to be owned fully or partly by a small super fund. There are advantages in having the property owned in a single super fund rather than partly in two funds, as it makes it easier to transfer the property over time between the business partners within one fund. With your business partner, you have aligned financial goals and objectives, and the super fund can assist you to support these while at the same time growing the investments of the fund for your retirement.

With any of these joint financial or working relationships, it's always important to have an eye on the exit. That's not to say you need to be pessimistic all the time about how things will work out, but it's important to know how you can resolve issues of conflict or differences of opinion.

Not only that, but you will also need to be considering what to do if you and your business partner are different in age. For example, if you are aged 45 and your business partner is aged 60, it is more than likely that your business partner will want to wind down their involvement or totally quit the business before you. What will that mean to you and to the business? If you still want to keep the business going, you will need to either pay out your partner or find a new business partner who can pay out your existing partner and take up their stake in the business. If there is insufficient planning or discussion about what both of you want to happen in those circumstances, the business could come to a screaming halt when the older partner wants out.

If the super fund holds the business property as an asset, you will also need to consider what happens with your fund and its investment. Your initial thoughts might be based around the retiring partner keeping their interest in the fund and continuing to enjoy the investment benefits of the property within their part of the super fund. However, as that person has ceased to be involved in the business, their degree of interest and passion for the property could wane over time.

This means that you will need to consider how your older business partner can receive their super payout from the fund without requiring the assets of the fund (including the business property) to be sold to do that. The options at that time will include:

- your new (incoming) business partner becoming a member of the fund to replace the outgoing business partner, providing cash to enable the super payout to be made
- ensuring that your fund is diversified with its investments, so that it is not necessary to sell the property to make the super payout, leaving you (as the ongoing business partner) with the property as an asset in your super fund
- involving other family members, including children, in both the business and the super fund, to ensure a continuity of the business and fund between generations.

Selling the property might be the only option in some circumstances, in which case the benefits of being the owner of the business property for your business pass to another party.

Remember that forward planning is very important when you have more than one member in your super fund, to ensure that you know how you can cope with the other members wanting to take their benefits out at some time in the future.

Your children

If it's good enough to have the next generation involved in the family business, you might think why not have the next generation involved in the family super fund? This is starting to add complications, and involving children needs more solid thinking before proceeding.

Involving children is less likely to be about their large balances adding to the pot of money to be invested, as they have not been involved in the superannuation system as long as you have.

Don't forget that a self-managed superannuation fund must have fewer than five members, which means that you can only have one, two, three or four members in your fund. If you and your spouse are members and you have more than two children, you can't fit all of your children into your fund. In these circumstances, you could only involve some of your children in the family fund.

Let's have a look at the pros and cons of having children in your super fund, which you will need to weigh up to see what is right for you and your fund.

The cons of having children in your super fund

Do your children have aligned or even similar financial goals to yours? How will they look at investing 'their money' in your fund? This potential lack of alignment is one of the most significant barriers to having your children in your own super fund.

Your children may not always be living in the same city, state or even country as you, so that would make it harder for them to be involved in running and making joint decisions about the family fund if they are remote from the rest of the family.

So, why would you want to have your children in your super fund? Some parents choose to involve their children in their family super fund as a means of educating them in financial issues and managing what is equivalent to a small business. However, this education process could just as efficiently be achieved by sharing the experience of the fund with your children without mandating their involvement. Remember that if they are members they must also be trustees or directors of the company trustee and are equally responsible for the activities of the fund.

As trustees, they have an equal vote with you. This means that if they have a different view on some of the fund's investments or activities, they may be able to block decisions about them. If there is a rift between parents and children, having them in the family super fund can be counter-productive all round.

The pros of having children in your super fund

But it's not all difficulties, and there are some very good reasons for inviting your children to be members of your super fund. Firstly, including your children as members of the fund provides a whole new source of additional money for investment, being their contributions and the transfer of existing super balances from other funds.

Furthermore, by enabling younger family members to participate in the fund and its decision-making at this time, there can be a gradual transfer of control and 'ownership' to the next generation. Their own balances in the fund become an important consideration, as children are generally unable to 'inherit' super within the same fund on the death of a parent. If the children have sufficient balances on the death of the parents, they may be able to retain key family investments within the fund, such as commercial property leased to the family business.

As the parents age, their ability or interest to manage the family super fund may decline, and it is important that there are others who can carry the load at that time. And finally, knowing what to do on the death of one or both of the parents is important, so much so that it is worth mapping this out now with your family, while you are still fit and well.

Resolving differences between fund members

While a prenuptial or financial agreement between partners or spouses can sound downright unromantic, the parties can find them very effective and useful in the event of a permanent breakdown of the relationship. In a similar way, it's important to have agreed rules in reserve for your super fund that can be triggered to resolve conflicts among the members of the fund.

In Australia, our family law legislation has specific provisions that enable superannuation to be divided between the parties in the event of separation, but with self-managed superannuation funds this requires the cooperation of both parties.

There are no specific legislative provisions that address what to do or how to resolve conflict if it occurs between members of a super fund who are business partners or parents and children, or siblings. That's why there needs to be provision for this to be addressed in the fund's trust deed, which sets out the rules for the fund.

What are the options for resolving differences? The different types of 'circuit breaker' include:

- having a 'principal' member of the fund who can instruct a member or members to remove themselves from the fund, taking their member balance to a new fund and ceasing to be a trustee as a result
- having an external dispute-resolution process that is binding on the trustees, where there is an agreed independent person who is appointed to mediate and potentially provide direction to resolve the conflict

- having some form of 'preferential voting' system with votes weighted in proportion to member balances – this feature is losing favour, with legal views suggesting that it is inconsistent with the provisions of general trust law.

The ATO as the regulator stays out of these disputes and sits on the side, unable to impose itself on the dispute. If the annual returns are not being lodged as a result of the dispute, the ATO has the right to apply penalties for non-lodgement or late lodgement.

This is a difficult area, and there has been significant expense incurred on legal fees in matters where trustees have been at loggerheads and unable to resolve their conflicts. Going to court is the ultimate means of resolving disagreements, but it is very expensive. If you end up in court, chances are that the lawyers will be the biggest winners.

It's a bit alarming to think it could get this messy, and that is why you are encouraged to think carefully before extending your fund beyond just yourself and your spouse. Don't say you haven't been warned!

That's enough of the negative stuff. What about some of the things you can think of when planning what you can do with your own super fund?

What happens when you retire?

What is 'retirement', anyway? Some people say it's just a frame of mind, while others regard a particular age as being the time to 'retire'. But as discussed in the opening chapters of this book, these days the concept of retirement is far broader, and 'financial independence' is perhaps a better way of looking at this stage of our lives.

In the Australian superannuation system, you are allowed to start taking some of your super balance as a regular income payment (a 'pension') when you reach preservation age. As we discussed in Chapter 1, for those born before 1 July 1960 this is age 55, and if you were born after 1 July 1964 it is age 60. If you were born somewhere in between, the preservation age is between 55 and 60.

That's the earliest you can start to take part of your money out of super, but you can leave all of your super balance intact without drawing against it well past age 65 if you don't have a need for additional money from your super. There is no compulsory retirement age when it comes to your super.

Figure 4.1 shows a 'typical' superannuation balance, which has two phases: accumulation and drawdown. The values are illustrative, and you can see that the balance continues to grow for a short time after the drawdown (pension) process starts, before progressively declining throughout retirement. We'll have another look at this figure later when we talk about investment strategies.

Figure 4.1: Superannuation Balance Across a Lifetime

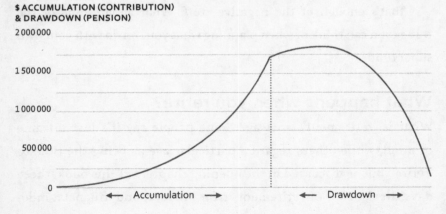

Just because you reach a particular 'retirement' age, it doesn't mean that you have to take all of your money out of super. On the contrary, you can continue to remain invested for a long period from that time onwards. In Australia, at age 65, the average remaining life expectancy is another 20–25 years, so it's not surprising that the balance continues to grow for a long time before gradually declining. Of course, full 'retirement' means that contributions are no longer being made to the fund, which means that the growth of your balance is derived only from investment earnings.

Some form of budgeting or business planning is useful when you have one or more members of the fund who are drawing against the fund for their pension payments. This is where having other members in the fund can work for you. As previously discussed, younger members of the fund will still have contributions being made to the fund, which can help with the cashflow and allow you to make pension payments from the fund without needing to sell down investments.

Super on the death of a fund member

What do you want your super to do on your death or the death of your spouse? Do you see it as providing an opportunity to provide money to your children to enable them to have greater financial comfort in their lives, or do you see it as an opportunity to enable them to continue with the 'family legacy' of investments in your super fund?

The way you approach your super fund and the strategies that are involved will be very different under these different options.

If you want to provide for your children after you and your spouse have died, you will want to see as little taxation as possible taken from the super benefits paid on your death. Your death benefits will be paid from your super fund after the assets have been sold and converted to cash.

Since the emphasis is on reducing the effect of taxation at the time of the death benefit being paid, your strategic thinking while you are alive and able to address this should be focused partly on the value of the wealth that you are creating and maintaining in your super fund, and partly on how you can improve the after-tax outcome. Chapter 9 covers some of the strategies that are followed to improve the tax outcome after death. Whatever strategies you put in place, you will need to ensure that there are clear directions left behind about the person or persons to whom you would like your death benefits to be paid.

It is not possible for your personal will to provide directions to the trustees of your fund as to whom your death benefits are to be paid. This must be documented under what is called a 'binding nomination', which specifies the person or persons to whom the super benefit should be paid. This is one of those 'supporting documents' that we spoke about earlier when talking about the trust deed for your fund.

If you want to use your super fund to create an investment legacy that can be continued by your children after your death and that of your spouse, the emphasis is less about tax planning and more about how you can ensure that the investments are retained in your (now 'their') super fund on your death. Remember that it is generally not possible (with limited exceptions for younger or dependent children) for your children to 'inherit' your or your spouse's super on your deaths.

'Family legacy' investments on death

If your death benefit needs to be paid from the fund, will there be sufficient member balances remaining to keep the asset or assets that you want to retain in the fund as 'family legacy' investments?

To illustrate this, if your fund has a commercial property that is being leased to the family business and that property is valued at $600 000, and there's also cash of $200 000, the fund has total assets of $800 000. If your account balance in the fund (that is, your death benefit) is $400 000 and the two children's account balances total $400 000, it's going to be difficult to retain the $600 000 property as an investment in the fund unless the fund can find another $200 000 in cash.

This could be solved by the two children each making a $100 000 cash contribution shortly after your death, which would produce a cash balance of $400 000. The fund would then have $400 000 in cash (the original $200 000 plus the $100 000 from each of the two children), which will be just enough to pay your death benefit of $400 000. The two children's total balances of $600 000 are now just covered by the value of the property. It's a finely balanced outcome and also assumes that the children can find that type of cash and are eligible to make that contribution to superannuation.

Such a big strategy needs a better chance of success than just hoping that the funds will be available to enable the contribution to be made by the children. It requires solid forward planning and open family discussion between parents and children, to ensure that you are all on the same page with the objective of maintaining the 'family legacy' within the super fund as much as possible.

You can change your emphasis or primary goal along the way, but the greater the period of time within which to work on the strategy, the better.

Any form of estate planning needs to be undertaken with all other components of your potential estate being identified, targeted and addressed in the will and associated documents.

Don't leave these to chance.

SUPER TIP

If you manage your own super fund, find out what happens with your benefits on your death. See if you have a binding nomination or some other nomination. If you don't understand what you have in place or can't find the documents, ask your trusted adviser.

If you are a member of a retail or industry super fund, have a look at your last annual member statement to see what nomination you have in place for your death benefits.

Check to see whether your current nominations remain relevant for your personal position.

Seek professional advice if you would like to change any of these nominations.

Where to now?

There's a lot to think about when you decide to have your own super fund, and it's important that you give sound consideration to these issues. It's a bit like building a house: you need to ensure that the foundations are properly constructed to ensure the long life of the house. The same applies for your super fund, and properly and completely addressing these issues will ensure you are more likely to have your super fund deliver the outcomes you would like.

Even the most committed 'do-it-yourselfer' is likely to benefit from some good professional advice and assistance in this area from a financial planner or accountant. Don't be hesitant to ask for help – after all, your financial future is at stake.

CHAPTER 5

The costs of DIY super

So what drives you when it comes to cost? Are you intent on having the lowest possible costs no matter what, or do you weigh up the cost against the value that comes from it? When you consider your super is likely to be one of the largest pots of money over which you have any influence (the others being your home and, possibly, your business), it's an important consideration.

How much super do you need to start your own fund?

The most common question that is raised about starting your own super fund is 'How much do I need to have my own super fund?' While there is no single correct answer to this question, a balance of $200 000 is often suggested as the minimum required to keep the fund at an economical cost per dollar invested. With annual costs of at least $800 per annum for a 'bare minimum' service (which we'll talk about later), a balance of much less than $200 000 could be more cost-effectively managed in an industry or retail fund, for example.

This is particularly relevant if you are influenced purely on a cost basis, but there might be other things that are motivating you to have your own super fund.

On the other hand, if the motivation to have your own super fund is to undertake unique investments or borrowing strategies that are not available in retail or industry funds, cost may be much less of an issue. If you really want to get into these unusual investment opportunities you might be prepared to run your own fund with a balance as low as $100 000, for example.

Don't forget that there's nothing wrong with starting off in a retail or industry fund and then moving on to your own super fund when you have enough money in it to justify the cost of setting up and running your own fund.

Leaving a working balance in your retail or industry fund

When you have enough to transfer into your new super fund, it could be worthwhile to leave a small balance in your existing retail or industry fund. You could then continue to have ongoing contributions made to that fund and then arrange for an end-of-year transfer of the majority of your balance into your own super fund, and repeat this each year.

Why do this? Well, it keeps the administration of your own fund much easier, as there is only one payment made into it each year and you don't need to worry about chasing and recording regular personal or employer contributions. It's all about considering whether you can have someone else do the hard work at a cheaper cost.

Another reason to consider leaving a balance in your retail or industry fund is that you might have existing insurance cover on your life that you don't want to lose. If you want to have insurance cover in your own super fund, you will need to arrange a new policy for that before you cancel your existing cover. This is an area where you should seek expert financial advice, to ensure that the terms of your current cover are properly replaced in the new insurance policy.

> **SUPER TIP**
>
> Have a look at your last super statement(s) and see how much insurance cover you have. This is the amount that will be added to your account balance if you die or become disabled. It's important that you consider whether this amount of cover is enough to meet any needs that you or your family might have if you die or become disabled. Talk to your adviser to discuss how much cover you should have.

Start-up costs

Having your own super fund means you can determine the level of services you want to seek from others and how much you want to do yourself. In the previous chapter, we discussed the trust deed for your fund and noted that the cheapest option is not always going to deliver the results you expect.

The choice of trustee structure is often driven by short-term cost, as it is much easier and cheaper to set up and maintain a fund with personal trustees rather than using a company as a trustee. However, there are more things that need attention and can go wrong if you have personal trustees. The hassle of adding or removing members and trustees can be significant when each asset holding needs to be updated to reflect the change of collective ownership. Proper recording of ownership of assets is one of the 'hot issues' that the ATO expects auditors to watch out for.

So, the choice of personal or company trustee is the first choice that involves cost versus value and convenience. For most people, the short-term burden of immediate cost dominates their thinking relative to the potential future additional value that comes from having a company as the fund's trustee. If your own super fund will have a large number of assets or property as an investment, it's a good idea to use the company trustee option, even if it costs a bit more. Take our word for it, this will save you time and money in the long run.

Is a cheap audit a good audit?

When selecting an auditor for your fund, the cost of the annual audit is likely to be one of the first issues raised. Make sure you know what the audit fee covers, and that there won't be any surprise extras along the way.

It's important that you should feel comfortable with your fund's auditor, as they will be the regulator's 'representative' when they undertake the audit of the fund's activities for the year and the end-of-year financial reporting.

What do you think is the role of your fund's auditor? Is it just to tick the boxes at the end of the year to confirm that everything about your fund is compliant, or is it to raise issues with you that might be a cause for concern at some time in the future? If you see the auditor as a valuable support resource, you should then be prepared to pay a higher audit fee than for an auditor that you want just to tick off the boxes. You need to talk with the auditor before you engage them to confirm what you want them to do – just do the year-end audit for example, or be available to answer questions on what you want to do properly during the year.

Cheap is not always good when it comes to making sure your fund is being run in accordance with the rules. Talk to your friends and your adviser about their experience with their auditor – a personal reference can give you better comfort than cheaper fees.

Keeping fund records

While super is quite straightforward and simple in the majority of cases, your fund needs to be maintained with the expectation that this will not always be the case. You need to remember that changes to superannuation law occur on a regular basis and that change is the constant. So it's important to keep records of the tax components of member benefits and to update these when benefits are paid or pensions are started. You also need to keep records of the cost base of assets to allow for the potential effect of capital gains tax, even though the fund may be currently supporting pensions.

If you are thinking of keeping the member and investment records yourself, it would be worthwhile talking to your appointed auditor before you get too far down that track of self-administration, to make sure you don't overlook some of the important records.

The majority of people who have DIY funds have their member and fund records updated or maintained by a professional administrator or accountant, rather than doing it themselves. Unless you are familiar with the accounting rules and standards, preparing end-of-year financial statements and annual reporting (including tax returns) can be very challenging – it is something probably best left to the professionals.

There is a whole range of service providers who can assist with the administration, record-keeping and preparation of end-of-year reporting for your fund. Your accountant will either provide this service or can refer you to an associated firm that will. As well as the accountants, there are specialist administration companies that provide these services. You can find them with an internet search.

SUPER TIP

Selecting a service provider for administration and record-keeping services is important. Talk to your accountant or your trusted adviser, or your friends, and ask if they have a suggested provider. Find out online, or ask them to provide you with information, about their fees and how much these services will be for your fund.

The more complicated your fund, the greater the cost of providing administration and record-keeping services. The higher the number of assets held and the higher the number of transactions that occur each year can influence your costs.

Cost of investing

The one common thread among those who have their own super fund is the desire to have a say in the investments of their own super fund. Having your own super fund means that the responsibility of deciding the assets of the fund is yours. We'll talk a bit later about how you go about setting an overall investment strategy, but within that strategy is the actual placement and management of the investments of your fund.

What level of involvement, for example, do you want with buying and selling listed shares? Do you want to buy and sell directly yourself – say, through an online broker – or do you want to involve a stockbroker in the trading activity?

Trading online yourself is simple and brokerage costs are low, but a stockbroker can give you helpful trading advice and make share trading in general easier for you.

There are choices available to you as to how you go about investing. If you want to buy and sell Australian shares yourself, and do your own research, there are a number of online share brokers you can use. The cost of these online brokers can be as low as $30 or 0.1% of the value of the shares traded (whichever is greater). If you want to receive advice and buy and sell shares through a stockbroker, the cost of these trades (and the associated advice) could be 1% or more of the value of the shares traded (and a minimum of $50).

For example, a $10 000 share trade is likely to cost you around $30 through an online broker, or around $100 using a full-service (advice-providing) stockbroker.

Advice and support

We'll talk about the investment process later, but you will need to consider whether you have appropriate expertise to determine the fund's ongoing investment portfolio. If you would like support with that there are a range of options available, from supplementary advice right through to using professional managers to manage parts of your super fund's portfolio.

As well as obtaining advice and support to assist you with the investment of your super fund's assets, you also need to consider how you will remain informed about the options that are available to you in your fund. These issues are often bundled under the general description of 'strategy'. This strategy can range from the mundane to the complex.

Doing your own research provides for the cheapest option, as there is little or no cost to obtaining information from newspapers, information seminars and the internet. There's lots of information out there on just about anything, as long as you know where to look and the key words to describe what you are looking to do, and as long as you know how to separate the good information from the bad (easier said than done). Also, as mentioned earlier, there is constant change in the super environment and this often brings the need to quickly review opportunities and problems.

What level of advice and support do you want to have for your fund? If you want to have issues identified as soon as they are relevant to you, this 'real-time' advice is likely to require an ongoing relationship with a financial adviser or accountant. It could be too late to address the opportunity if you wait for the end of the year to investigate it. Furthermore, if you decide that a specific action or strategy needs to be undertaken, it's important that it's done in a manner that is not only consistent with super law, but also with the trust deed.

Make sure that the adviser you use explains to you why they are suggesting you undertake certain actions or strategies. A good adviser should be educating you along the way, so that your knowledge and understanding grow over time.

You should never assume that there are no further issues or strategies you can take on for your own super fund. Your super fund is about more than just today and yourself – it is about a long-term investment and ongoing support to you and your family. This involves a dynamic process, as it is influenced by many changing issues along the way.

Fixed and variable cost – it's about what you need

The two 'fixed' services for your fund are the trust deed and audit. All of the other services are 'variable', depending on the degree of 'DIY' that you are looking to achieve.

For each of the services, whether 'fixed' or 'variable', the fees vary significantly. Under the 'variable' services, the level of support and advice that you arrange also affects the fees you pay. This means that you need to do some homework on the alternatives available in each service segment to determine which is likely to be most appropriate for you.

Also, remember that while you might want to minimise costs and fees, cheap does not necessarily mean that you will get the best long-term value for the money spent. That said, as you move up the service-provider cost chain make sure that the additional cost that you incur does lead to greater value for you and your super fund.

One of the reasons for using advisers is not only to keep you well informed, but also to keep you out of jail.

CHAPTER 6

Keeping inside of the law

It's your super fund and it's your money, so you can do what you want with it. If you think that, you're wrong! Think again. Anyone who is considering setting up their own super fund or using their own super fund with the intention of deliberately breaking the rules should think seriously about what they are doing and the consequences of their actions. You will get caught.

There's a big difference between breaking the rules and knowing what the rules are and working within them, even if that means pushing it right to the legal limit. That's where strategic advice and support can come in handy.

We have previously spoken about the means by which small super funds are monitored, which is through an annual audit by an independent auditor who is responsible for confirming that the fund has been run in accordance with the legal requirements. Any breaches of the law are required to be reported on the annual return and these are then investigated by the regulator, the Australian Taxation Office (ATO).

What are the major offences?

There are some really serious offences that are right at the top of the hit list for the regulator. These relate to having a 'disqualified person' as a trustee, and to 'early release' of funds.

We spoke earlier in Chapter 4 about the requirements for being a trustee of a super fund, and in particular that a trustee cannot be a 'disqualified person'. Remember that a disqualified person is a person who fits into one of the following categories:

- has been convicted of an offence relating to dishonest conduct
- is an undischarged bankrupt
- has been penalised for breaching one of the major superannuation rules
- has been disqualified by the regulator.

Running a fund with a disqualified person as a trustee is going to get you into serious trouble with the Tax Office. Given the avalanche of information that is out there on the internet and the data sharing that goes on between government departments, the chance of detection if you have a disqualified person as a trustee is increasing all the time. It's not worth the risk.

Inviting a person to be a trustee of your super fund without checking with them about their status as a 'disqualified person' is asking for trouble. They must make a declaration about their status at the time of taking on their role as trustee, so don't forget to see that this is done at that time. But it's not only at the time each trustee starts, it's important to recheck with your fellow trustees that nothing has occurred after they started as a trustee that would place them in a 'disqualified person' category. It's good practice to require that each trustee make at least an annual declaration that they are not a disqualified person, and to record that in the regular trustee minutes. If this is done and it still turns out that one of your fellow trustees was actually a disqualified person, you might be excused for having sought that information and having been misinformed by the offending trustee.

By not asking you could be regarded as being negligent, and therefore also open to penalty.

The other major offence relates to what is called 'early release', which is where moneys are paid out from the super fund before the law allows that to occur. There are people who promote the early release of super moneys and the Tax Office works tirelessly to find the promoters of these schemes and to punish them with penalties and jail sentences.

Unfortunately, their 'victims' are also penalised, as the trustees who allowed their super funds to release these amounts have also committed an offence. Their offence was not only to break the law, but also, more importantly, was to not be familiar with the key requirements and regulations relating to super.

If someone tells you that they can get money out of your super fund ahead of time, don't fall for it. What they are talking about is illegal, and they will often charge a large fee for what they propose to do. That alone should indicate that there is something amiss.

When you have your own super fund and become a trustee of the fund, you are undertaking that you will run your fund in accordance with the rules – so it's important that you either know the rules or engage with a trusted adviser or supporter who can ensure that you don't break them.

What are the most common rules that are broken?

According to the report prepared for the review of the superannuation system, called the Cooper Review, published in 2010, two-thirds of the offences that were picked up in the annual audits were in four main areas:

1. Providing loans / financial assistance to members

You can't lend money from your fund to a member of your family no matter what the circumstances – even for short periods.

If your super fund owns a commercial property that is used by a business run by a member of the fund, you must ensure that the rental payments paid by the business are paid on time and in the correct amount, just as you would if the property was being used by a total stranger. If you don't chase up late or missing rental payments, this is treated as if you had provided a financial advantage, or assistance, to the family member's business.

It's often tempting to turn a blind eye to family members who are late with their company's rent or don't pay the appropriate amount, but you can't do that in this case, as it breaks one of the rules of investment of super funds.

2. Administration

You can't afford to get sloppy with the administration of your super fund. Make sure that you have your fund's annual returns audited and lodged well before the due date for the year. For funds that have been around for more than 12 months, the due date of these annual returns is normally 15 May of the year following the end of the financial year. This provides ample time to get the fund's records for the year in order, have the financial reports and tax return prepared, have the fund audited and, finally, arrange for the lodgement of the annual returns.

It's surprising, but only 70% of small funds lodge on time, with the remaining 30% being late for one reason or another. That's one way of attracting the attention of the regulator and possibly causing your time to be wasted with 'please explain' letters or, even worse, an audit from the Tax Office. You might not have anything to hide, but it takes up your time or your accountant's time (and your money).

Don't forget to keep good records of the decisions you make as trustee of your super fund. For example, if you decide that you want to start a pension in your fund after you have reached the required age, it's important that you have written records of the member's request to start the pension and the trustee's agreement to do so. These records are generally set out in the form of trustee minutes.

The law requires that you keep the fund's records for at least 10 years. This means that you need to know where the records are just in case you are audited by the Tax Office. It's just like keeping records when you are in business.

3. In-house assets

There are two main requirements relating to the investment of your fund's money. First, you need to set down a strategy that governs how you intend to invest your fund's money. This strategy will confirm the types of assets that the fund can invest in, as well as the purpose of investing in these assets.

Second, with limited exceptions (which relate to what are known as 'in-house assets'), all investments must be placed on an 'arms-length' basis. By 'arms-length', we mean that the investment has terms and conditions that would be agreed on and accepted by two people who are unrelated, or are strangers.

This leaves quite an extensive range of investments that can be used by super funds, with the main ones including:

- bank accounts
- term deposits

- shares in listed companies
- complex investment arrangements (such as options or futures) relating to these shares
- shares in private (unlisted) companies
- managed investment funds
- property (commercial or residential)
- loans to third parties
- unit trusts.

These are just the simple types of investments that are undertaken in small funds. Effectively, any investment that can be undertaken on a private basis is likely to be able to be achieved in a small super fund. Chapter 7 covers how borrowed money can be used to invest within a small-fund context.

There are restrictions on how an asset can be bought or transferred from a related party. The only types of asset that can be bought or transferred from a related party are listed shares and business property. It's important to get this right and you should seek expert advice from your adviser before considering buying or transferring an asset from a related party.

So what's the special deal with an 'in-house asset'? An 'in-house asset' is defined[1] as being an asset that is:

- a loan to, or investment in, a related party[2] of the fund
- an asset (other than commercial property) that is the subject of a lease or lease arrangement with a related party of the fund
- an investment in a related trust of the fund.

---

1 Refer to Section 71 of the Superannuation Industry Supervision Act 1993 for the full detail.
2 A 'related party' has specific meaning under the law and a very wide definition that includes relatives or business associates of the member, or the spouse of any of these people, as well as businesses that are controlled by those people.

There's nothing wrong with having one or more of these in-house assets, if they are held in accordance with the investment strategy. However, there is a limit on how much of your fund's assets can be held in these in-house assets – no more than 5%, in fact. This means that in-house assets can only be held if they represent less than 5% of the value of the fund's total assets.

This is good news at least, as it means that the rules allow you to make loans to your own business or a related business – but only within that 5% limit. Sure, the loan must have arms-length terms and conditions (such as the rate of interest and repayment terms), but the 5% limit is in place to reduce the risk of your fund being too heavily exposed to one single investment that is tied up with your own or a related business – to avoid having too many eggs in the one basket that is close to home.

It's not surprising that this is a common problem area, as it is often where boundaries are pushed and pushed. It's often tempting to want to advance loans in excess of the 5% limit to related businesses, when they are struggling over the short term. Going over the 5% limit is illegal. This limit is there to protect you, since if the business goes under you don't want to run the risk of losing too much of your super – particularly at a time that it might be even more important support for you. So you can't risk too much of your super with your business. It's surprising how many funds are caught loaning too much (more than 5% of their fund) to their family's businesses. Don't be one of them.

4. Asset ownership

It's important that you keep good records for your super fund, and that includes records of the assets the fund holds. When you make an investment with your fund's money, the asset should be properly recorded as being owned by the trustee of the fund.

The law requires that there must be a clear separation of ownership of the assets of your super fund from any other assets you might own. The reason for this is fairly clear: you want to ensure that your super assets are protected from any claim by creditors against your own assets.

If asset ownership is not clear, it can also cause confusion on the death of one of the members, with the executor of their estate trying to determine which assets are personally owned (and form part of the estate) and which belong to the super fund.

Proper recording of the ownership of the super-fund assets ensures that the ownership of these assets is clearly set down. So where do the problems occur?

The main problem comes with funds that have personal trustees. If you have a small fund with personal trustees, it's important that the assets are listed as being owned by you (and your fellow trustees) in your capacity as trustee of your super fund. For example, 'John Smith and Mary Smith as trustees for the Smith Superannuation Fund'. If the asset is just listed as being owned by 'John Smith', there is no clear sign that it is a super-fund asset as opposed to one that is owned by John Smith personally. The same goes when you have a company as trustee. The assets should be listed as being owned by 'Smith Super Pty Ltd as trustee for the Smith Superannuation Fund', to make it absolutely clear who owns them.

Remember that if there is any uncertainty or confusion about who owns an asset, it will take time and money to confirm that it really belongs to your super fund. You may not be there to provide an explanation at the time. Getting this bit right can save a lot of pain and bother later, for your surviving family members.

The key message from these common problem areas is that the rules that are set down in the law and in your fund's trust deed are there to protect you, so it's important that you know what they are and make sure you don't break them.

What happens if you break the rules?

The answer to this question is 'Plenty' – and it's not pleasant. There are serious consequences for breaking the rules.

The current system has a range of fines and penalties if rules are broken. The level of the penalty depends on the seriousness of the rule or rules that have been broken, and multiple penalties can be applied for related breaches.

The most significant penalty that can be applied is for your fund to be made 'non-complying', which means that the regulator has tried to work with you to fix all of the legal breaches but you have not chosen to cooperate. Aside from the monetary penalties and fines that can be imposed, a non-complying fund suffers the highest rate of personal tax (that's around 47 cents in the dollar) against the total balance of the fund. This penalty is recognised as being a very harsh one, and is only applied by the Tax Office in the most extreme circumstances, where the fund trustees have persistently failed to remedy their breaches.

To consider what this penalty is equivalent to, it's like crushing the car of a driving offender for a serious offence – a very extreme punishment that would need to fit the extremity of the offence. But when you are driving a car, there are a range of rules you need to follow to ensure that the road is a safe place for all users and pedestrians. If these rules are broken and you are caught, there are consequences that are proportionate to the degree of the offence. The fine for speeding at less than 15 kilometres over the limit, for example, is less than the fine for speeding at more than 30 kilometres over the limit. If you drive through a red-light speed camera in excess of the speed limit as well as through the red light, you can be fined for both offences at the same time. The same applies for offences by trustees of their own small super funds.

Examples of fines[3] (in financial year 2013/2014) are:

- not keeping fund records for 10 years: $1700
- not providing details of change of trustees to the regulator: $3400
- lending money to a member or relative: $10 200.

The fines for breaking the super rules cannot be paid from the assets of the fund, but must be paid by the trustee personally, so any super penalties will hit your hip pocket.

Don't forget that penalties are applied against each of the trustees – which could include you – if rules are broken, even if you might not have known about what was happening at the time. This drives home the need for you, as a trustee, to stay on top of what is happening in your super fund, and to ensure that everything is being done correctly and legally.

The regulator can also instruct the trustees to undertake an online training program if they believe that the trustees are not properly familiar with their responsibilities. Not attending or completing such a program carries its own penalty.

It's just not worth trying to run your fund without being properly aware of all of the rules and requirements. Seek advice if you are not sure.

Offences by your fellow trustees

Be careful whom you invite to join you as a trustee in your own super fund. You are responsible for what they do as a trustee of your fund.

---

3 These fines were proposed to be implemented for the 2013/2014 year, but had not yet been legislated at the time of writing.

There have been reported cases where parents allowed their (mature-aged) child to join their family super fund and included the child as a signatory of the super fund's bank account, only to find that the child has then removed the cash for their own purposes. While the child was caught and penalised, the parents were unable to restore the withdrawn moneys and were penalised as trustees of the fund for allowing funds to be withdrawn inappropriately.

SUPER TIP

If you want to invite other family members into your fund, think about what you should do about the signatories to the fund's bank account. It's quite okay to require that all payments must be made with two signatures, one of which is yours. This cuts the chances of other family members taking money out of your fund without your permission.

We spoke earlier about the problems that can occur when family relations break down and you have a husband and wife in the same fund as trustees. It's difficult for both parties to keep an eye on the super fund at all times, but it's important if you are a trustee of a super fund not to be a passive trustee, so take an interest and ensure that you can see what is going on. Have a look at bank statements as they come in or go online and monitor them.

Paying attention to detail

It's not just the 'black and white' rules you need to monitor to ensure that you don't fall outside the law. You also need to keep an eye on some of the 'softer' rules, which can have taxation consequences for you or your fund. These relate to contributions and pensions.

Let's look at contributions first. There are limits on the amount of contributions that you can make or your employer can make on your behalf before you start to incur penalty tax. These were discussed in Chapter 2. It's not against the rules for contributions to be made above these limits, but you can be hit with a bill for additional tax when your contributions in a financial year are too high (above the annual caps). And to make it more complicated, there are special rules that allow for higher personal contributions to be made under special 'three-year' rules.[4]

If you fall outside these limits or rules you could lose some of your hard-earned super contributions in penalty tax. It's important to know the rules and know how you are travelling against them. Having your own super fund means that the buck stops with you in keeping an eye on the contributions that have been made by or for you during each financial year.

Similar comments can be made about the payment of pensions from your fund. In Chapter 2 we spoke about the requirement that you must make payments from your pensions of at least the specified minimum level.[5]

What happens if you don't make payments at the minimum level? At its very simplest, your fund will pay higher tax as it will not have met the pension conditions for that pension. This can be a very expensive error, since the investment income for the year will now be subject to tax, on both realised capital gains (for assets sold during the year) and income earned during the year.

---

4 Up to age 65, you can make personal contributions of up to $150 000 in any year. These 'non concessional' contributions do not attract contributions tax. Under the 'three year rule', it is possible to make non-concessional contributions of up to $450 000 in a three-year period.
5 Have another look at the table in Chapter 2, which shows that the minimum annual pension is 4% of your super balance up to age 65, and higher at older ages.

SUPER TIP

If you are paying pensions from your fund, make sure you know what the required minimum payments are in each financial year and that they are paid well before the end of the financial year. Don't leave it too late to make the payments.

Being aware of what you need to keep an eye on for your super fund will help you go a long way to paying the right amount of tax, saving as much of your money for your retirement as possible, and not giving it unnecessarily to the Tax Office.

Beware the spruikers

It's not only the Tax Office that you need to be worried about – there is also the risk of losing your hard-earned retirement savings to investment spruikers. One of the best investment sayings is 'If it sounds too good to be true, then it is', and this certainly applies to investment spruiking. The explosion in the number of small super funds has been accompanied by an even faster growth in the number of cheats and swindlers out there who are trying to get their hands on your hard-earned money.

Recognising that this represents a large risk to the superannuation system, the Australian Federal Police has set up a specific unit to monitor the activities of these investment promoters around small super funds. Unfortunately, that unit is growing.

These investment promoters are exploiting two everyday character traits: greed and trust. People who run their own super fund are likely to have larger amounts available for investing than average members of the community, and their motivation is most often to improve their own financial position. Even the better educated can fall victim to investment scammers, so you need to be alert.

Reputable investment providers do not make cold calls to your home or business, nor do they try to rush you to make a quick decision to invest funds with them. If you are contacted by phone by one of these investment promoters, try asking the following questions and see what answers you get.

'Why did you phone me and how did you get my number?' If their response is that it was your bank, rest assured that your bank would never provide your contact details to an external party as it is illegal to do so – so don't fall for that one.

'Can you please send me something in writing so that I can consider the opportunity more completely?' Of course the scammers will not provide you with anything in writing as that would leave a trail for the company and the regulator of investment advisers, ASIC.

Perhaps the best question, which shows that you have some knowledge of the Australian investment system, is 'What is your AFSL number?' An AFSL is the Australian Financial Services Licence, which must be quoted on demand by an authorised provider of investment advice.

If you think it might be a scam, it probably is. Ask for their details and contact number on the basis that you then can contact them when it is convenient to you. If they give them to you, try doing an internet search to see if they have a public profile, or go to the ASIC-related websites and look at the scams area.

These are generally clever people who are preying on the under-informed and unwary, so don't become yet another victim.

Watch out for identity fraud

Another area of criminal activity with investments and money is identity fraud. You can reduce your chances of becoming an innocent victim by taking some simple steps. The underlying principle is that you should protect your super-fund records and information in the same way that you would protect your personal tax and employment information.

Don't provide details of your fund's bank account to third parties unless they have a reason to need it, such as the Tax Office (to pay a tax refund) or the share registry (to pay share dividends). If someone wants to deposit funds, they can mail you a cheque if you don't feel comfortable giving them details of your bank account.

The public records for your fund only provide the suburb of the fund's registered address and Australian Business Number (ABN), and they do not include details of its Tax File Number (TFN). There should be no need to disclose your fund's TFN unless it is to a financial provider such as a bank or share registry, so that you can avoid paying withholding tax.

If your super fund's bank account has online access, make sure the password is a difficult one and don't keep it with the fund's paper records. Your super fund can have a lot of cash in the bank from time to time, so don't leave this at risk of online theft. There's a lot more at risk through your super fund than there is with your personal bank accounts.

It's a big world out there and there are lots of people who are looking to rip you off if you give them the opportunity.

But what about the decent people who run good investment businesses? Can your fund lose with them?

What happens if a good investment goes bad?

Unfortunately, there are many stories of well-run investment businesses that go to the wall, including through stretching themselves too thin or as a result of internal fraud within their own operations.

How can you protect your own fund against that? You can work with a licensed adviser who can provide you with options for investing your super money, and an explanation of the different types of investments and their risks.

For the controllers, you just can't beat obtaining detailed information about an investment and having a good read of the detail to understand how the investment works and how it makes money. If you find the detail too difficult to follow, then should you use it within your fund? It's good advice worth following that if you can't understand how an investment works or is supposed to work, you shouldn't touch it. Similarly, if you can't explain what an investment is about to your fellow super-fund trustees, you should walk away from it and not try to rope them into it.

There are countless assets you can invest in – just discard from the list any you can't understand. There are plenty of others available that you can understand, and if you're going to invest, they're the ones to look at. While you should do as much homework as possible when considering an investment, you can never be sure how it will pan out, and even the seemingly better investments can experience problems.

If an investment does go bad, all you can do is to sit back and wait for it all to be resolved by a liquidator or professional administrator. If this happens, you have the same rights as the next investor and each person has equal standing, even though your holding might represent a hefty portion of your super fund.

For the larger super funds and the small funds that are regulated by APRA (remember the 'small APRA funds'?), superannuation law provides for a protection system in the unfortunate event that an investment manager fails and there is a widespread effect on a large number of members of one or more of these funds. That protection results in the members of the other APRA regulated super funds paying a levy to assist in bailing out the members of the fund that were adversely affected by the failed investment manager. This arrangement is only available to APRA-regulated funds, not small self-managed super funds.

So why does this protection system not apply to small super funds that are regulated by the Tax Office? The first reason is that trustees of the APRA-supervised funds are different from the members of those funds, and these trustees are making a selection of investment products on behalf of the members of the funds.

Members of APRA-supervised funds do not have a direct say in which investments are made available for their use within the fund. These members are therefore protected in the event that the trustees have selected an investment that subsequently fails, even though it might have been heavily scrutinised by the fund trustee.

The second reason is that the protection is funded by a levy against members of all other APRA-regulated funds, even though these funds were not invested with the failed investment product. There is no choice about being in the protection system for the APRA-regulated funds or about paying the levy when it is called up by APRA. However, a large proportion of the small self-managed super funds may not have any investment in managed funds or managed investments that are the subject of this protection arrangement. If some small self-managed super funds don't have these types of investments, it would be unreasonable for them to be required to pay a levy with no possibility that they might be protected at some future stage. It would not be acceptable to the majority of small funds to have an additional levy (i.e. cost) for this protection when they might never benefit from it.

So, is there any remedy for small funds when an investment goes bad? Well, one way is to participate in legal action through the courts to seek recovery of some of the losses. In some cases, the losses can be recouped from insurance that the investment manager had in place, but in the majority of cases the legal action is taken against the principals, board and senior management of the investment company. When you get down to that level, the chance of obtaining much of a recovery is small.

It's therefore very important to do your homework with the investments of your super fund and make sure that you understand how the investments work and how they earn money for you.

Don't forget that it's your money in your super fund, so don't be lazy with how you keep your fund's records and how you make decisions about your fund and its investments. Having your own super fund requires you to make more decisions than when you use a retail or industry super fund, but that's why you have your own fund – because you like that hands-on approach to your super.

When you're managing your own super, there's no one else to blame for your decisions – the buck stops with you.

CHAPTER 7

Borrowing to invest through your DIY fund

DIY super funds are able to combine two powerful forces – borrowing and the tax-privileged superannuation system – to work together to provide small-fund investors with additional returns. Here we're talking about borrowing to buy property, which is part of the Australian investment psyche, as well as borrowing to buy shares. We'll talk about these two types of investments separately, since the rules affect them differently.

But before you get too excited, don't forget why you decided to have your own super fund, which was to achieve a better return on your money and to enjoy this in your retirement.

There are three issues that need to be considered when borrowing through super:

- having your own super fund
- investing in property or shares
- using borrowing to support investments.

Together they are powerful, but you need to be able to tick each one off separately before proceeding. Issues relating to having your own super fund have already been covered. This chapter focuses on investing in property and shares, and using borrowing to support investments.

Property as your super-fund investment

Super funds are able to buy most types of property. There are, however, some restrictions on buying property from family and business associates, and regarding who can rent a residential property from your super fund.

Just because you want to use borrowed funds does not change these rules. You can't use borrowed funds through super to buy a residential property and then live in it – it's very much against super rules. If you do want to buy a residential property and live in it, you have to do that outside of super.

As we have spoken about earlier in the book, it's okay for your own business or a related business to lease a commercial property that is owned by your super fund. Just make sure that the lease payments are made on a market basis to ensure that the property is not treated as an 'in-house asset'.

As for the property you choose to buy through your super fund, just like any property you may consider investing in, you should only invest if you are fully comfortable with the quality of the property and the ongoing lease or rental return that it will provide to your super fund. Don't forget that if your property is without a tenant for some time its rental income stops and your expenses continue, so make sure that you are buying a property that will be well sought after by tenants.

It's good practice to have an independent person whose opinion you respect, such as a good family friend or business associate, look over the property with you prior to purchase – just as you may have done when buying your first home. Why should your super fund's investment in property be any different?

If you already own a commercial property outside your super fund you can arrange for the fund to buy that property from you (either with cash from the fund or using borrowed funds). Alternatively, you can arrange for the property to be contributed to the fund as an in-specie contribution. This allows a property to be moved into super, without the fund needing to pay for the property.

If you are considering using a commercial property as a contribution, it's a good idea to first seek expert advice to make sure that your plans will not result in unexpected tax penalties. This relates to the contribution caps discussed in earlier chapters.

If you're buying a new property with borrowed funds, it needs to be a good-quality property that will deliver the returns you need to meet the cost of borrowing and will then provide good long-term value.

Borrowing to buy property

Do you remember when you bought your first house and the 'huge' mortgage that went with it? Do you remember the feelings that you had at the time – is it the right thing to do, how will I ever repay the debt, what if something goes wrong?

You should experience the same feelings if you are borrowing to buy a property in your super fund (except you will not be living in it if it is a residential property).

There are two key reasons why people borrow to invest:

• they don't have enough money to make an investment outright (that is, a shortfall in available capital)

• to use existing money to achieve a higher return (that is, leveraging existing capital).

The shortfall in capital is an issue when you have identified a particular property as being an appropriate investment for your super fund but you don't have enough spare cash to buy it. Leveraging (or 'gearing') existing capital enables you to look for much larger properties with your available capital, to achieve a greater or magnified future return on your money.

However, just because you can borrow inside your super fund doesn't mean you have to.

Don't be pressured

Have you ever wondered how it is that when the majority of the public thinks the property market is down, real estate agents are the only ones talking it up? There is always a good time to be buying property according to these guys, and that time is – now! Real estate agents must be the most optimistic people that I know.

With this permanent positive sentiment throughout the real estate industry, don't get pressured into buying property in your super fund. The media is full of 'good news' opportunities for investing in property and this will always be the case. You need to remember that real estate salespeople are remunerated based on sales and need to remain focused on their next success. If you are considering buying a property, seek out expert advice to ensure that the property will suit your super fund and your stage of life.

Furthermore, banks and lending institutions are continually looking for the next loan and will therefore be actively promoting the ability to use borrowed funds to buy property. So don't be surprised if you hear a real estate agent or bank teller asking if you have considered borrowing to buy property or borrowing through super to buy property – it's their job to raise the opportunity with you.

Borrowing from a bank

The banks have been behaving much more conservatively since the global financial crisis, which began in 2007, than they did before. Their shareholders (which might include your own super fund, incidentally) want to obtain a good return on their investment and generally don't want to see higher risk.

When taking out a loan to borrow through your super fund, the same issues come up as when you apply for a personal mortgage.

1. Loan-to-valuation ratio

The loan to valuation ratio, or LVR, is the proportion of the value of the property that the bank is prepared to lend you. A higher LVR is generally available for property that is regarded as less risky to the bank, such as residential property. Commercial property has a lower LVR, as it can often have restrictions on use due to zoning or specific-purpose premises.

It's unusual to see LVRs in excess of 80% for residential property and much above 70% for commercial property, although individual banks may differ depending on their knowledge of the particular property.

The higher the LVR, the greater the risk to the bank that the loan may not be fully recovered in the event of a decline in the value of the property.

2. Loan default

In the event of default on the loan, the bank will want to recover its loaned funds. There are specific superannuation rules that require that the borrowing of the super fund is 'limited recourse', which means that the bank cannot use any other assets of the super fund for security – only the property that is the subject of the borrowing.

This increases the risk to the bank, and it is common for them to apply a higher rate of interest to partly lay off this additional risk, as well as requiring that personal guarantees be given by the trustees of the super fund.

3. Rates of interest

Let's not forget that banks are in business to make money, so if they regard you as a higher risk they will charge you a higher rate of interest. Don't expect to borrow at personal-mortgage rates through your super fund. You should expect a figure somewhere between personal-mortgage rates and secured commercial rates for your super-fund borrowing.

Make sure you shop around for a good rate of interest, and don't be caught out by a low honeymoon rate followed by a higher ongoing rate. Do your homework and look around.

You can select a fixed or variable rate according to where you think we are in the interest-rate cycle. Whether to fix or use variable rates is an important decision, and you will need to consider the risks to your fund's returns from the overall investment before making it.

4. Interest coverage and loan servicing

The bank will want to see how you will be able to meet the ongoing interest cost as well as how you will be able to gradually service the debt (that is, reduce the amount outstanding) over the time of the loan.

Look at the cash flow position of your super fund to see where the money will come from. What will happen if the tenants leave and the property is vacant for three months or six months, or even longer?

Is the fund receiving ongoing contributions that will enable the borrowing to be serviced and repaid over time?

If these questions have a familiar ring to them, that's not surprising as these are the same issues that you needed to consider with your first (and subsequent) home purchase.

5. Personal guarantees

We spoke earlier about the banks only having recourse in the event of default against the property that is the subject of the borrowing. To provide a higher level of protection, the banks will often require personal guarantees to be given by the trustees in the event of loan default. This enables them to come after the individual trustees and force them to make up the balance of the loan out of their personal assets if the property is sold for less than the loan balance.

It's surprising how easily personal guarantees are given over borrowings, whether mortgages or super-fund borrowings, but they can have a major effect on the individual if they are called up when the borrower defaults.

If you are asked to go guarantor for family or friends for their personal borrowings, make sure you know what you are letting yourself in for. It's your personal money that can be at risk. The same applies to going guarantor for your super fund's borrowing.

Insuring the property

You've spent all that time and money and bought the property, so don't forget to make sure that it is insured. It's no different from insuring your own home, and you want to cover any risks that could reduce the value of your investment.

The lease contract or agreement with the tenant will confirm who is responsible for taking out insurance for each of the risks, so don't overlook this.

Borrowing to invest in shares

So far we have only spoken about borrowing to buy property, but is there any other type of asset that can be bought with borrowed funds? A qualified yes is the answer.

Borrowing that involves using funds loaned by a bank or other source to buy an asset or assets is much easier when investing in property. It is possible to use borrowed funds to buy shares, but there are some restrictions under the super borrowing rules that make this a bit hard (not impossible, just hard):

- Borrowed funds can be used to buy shares in one company only, so if you want to borrow to buy shares in more than one company you need to have different loans and different trusts set up for each company share parcel you want to buy.
- If you want to sell parcels of some of the shares, you need to arrange for the loan to be repaid at that time – you can't keep the borrowing in place if you sell one or more shares.
- If you want to sell the shares and buy new ones, you will need to repay the first loan and take out a new loan for the new shares.

It's not impossible, just hard to work with borrowed funds to invest in shares under these rules. However, borrowing to invest in shares can be undertaken more simply using special types of investments called 'instalment warrants', which involve what is called 'internal borrowing'. Each instalment warrant is a single share with its own borrowing, all wrapped up together.

Instalment warrants are generally related to high-quality listed shares, with the initial investment being used to purchase a portion of the underlying share, and future dividends used to meet the borrowing cost for the balance. If the value of the underlying share increases over the term, the instalment warrant leads to a capital profit to the investor. As with any form of geared investment, if the underlying share loses value, the overall transaction can result in a net loss being made.

Instalment warrants are available in some retail and industry super funds, since this form of borrowing in super can be undertaken across all types of superannuation funds that offer their members a choice of investments, and that includes instalment warrants on their menu of choices. Of course in your own fund you determine the menu from which to select, so instalment warrants are always available. Direct borrowing to buy property or shares (not using instalment warrants) is only available in small funds of fewer than five members.

The law

Borrowing inside super funds has a short history, with the law first being changed in 2007 to permit super funds to borrow for the purpose of investing.

It has always been possible, and continues to be so, for all super funds to borrow in a temporary capacity for the following purposes:

- for up to 90 days, to enable the payment of a benefit to a fund member
- for up to seven days to cover settlement of on-market investment purchases, where the need to borrow was not expected at the time of the investment decision being made.

In both cases, the borrowing must be for less than 10% of the assets of the fund.

These are pretty limited circumstances, and they are not likely to trouble you most of the time.

The rules relating to borrowing to undertake investments in a super fund have undergone major changes since they were introduced in 2007, and you should expect that to continue. With the rules continually changing, it's important to stay on top of them – this is done most easily by regular consultation with your professional financial adviser – if you are thinking of borrowing to make a property or share investment in your super fund.

The rules make it clear that borrowing can only be used to buy a new asset, and it is not possible to borrow funds using an existing super-fund asset as security.

If you are not sure about whether you can do something in this area, it's vital to ask an expert as the penalty for getting it wrong can be heavy. Not only can you be subject to penalties under the legislation if you borrow outside the rules, but you might also be required to sell the asset to remedy the problem, which could result in a poor short-term return for you.

Fund rules

So we know that the law allows super funds to borrow to invest in property and shares, but what about the rules of the fund itself, under the trust deed?

Just because the law says that you can borrow, that's not the end of the story – your trust deed needs to specifically allow you to borrow to invest. If your trust deed doesn't allow borrowing to invest, get it changed before you go any further with your borrowing strategy.

Don't forget that your fund needs to have a formal investment strategy that sets out the parameters within which the trustee intends to invest the assets of their fund. Have a look at the investment strategy to see if it allows you to invest in property or shares. If it does not allow that, it's time to bring it up to date. You can change your investment strategy at any time, but make sure you are investing in accordance with the strategy – otherwise, the auditor will report that you are not following your strategy.

Finally, does the investment strategy contemplate that the trustee can borrow to invest in property or shares? If not, fix it before you borrow. The bank is likely to want to see the investment strategy as part of their due-diligence process.

Ownership of the investment property or shares subject to borrowing

If you have borrowed to invest in property or shares through your super, the property or shares are not fully owned by the super fund or the bank while the borrowing is in place. The way that it is undertaken is set out in Figure 7.1.

Figure 7.1: Illustration of Super Property Borrowing

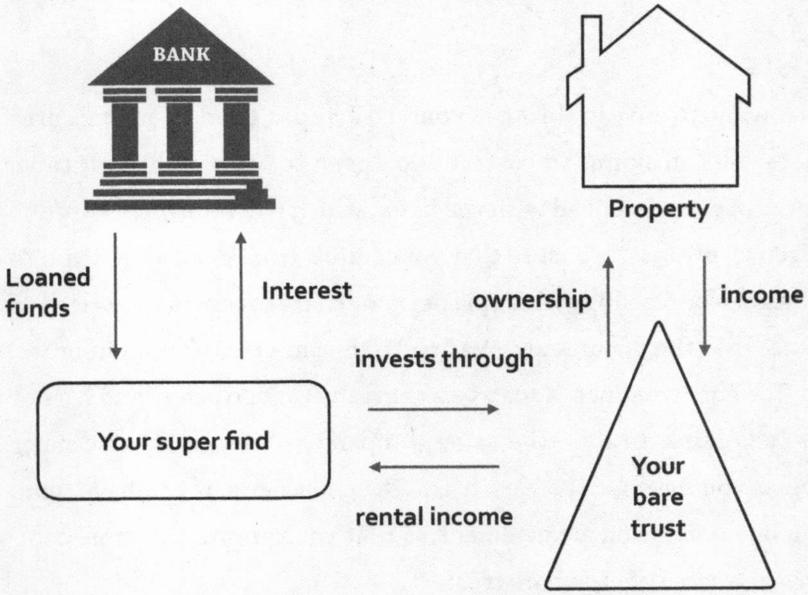

The trustee of the super fund is responsible to the bank for repaying the borrowing and meeting the ongoing interest payments. The super fund receives the ongoing rental income from the property or dividends from the shares, which helps to meet the interest cost.

The property or shares are held in a separate trust, called a 'bare trust', which means that the trust is holding the property or shares on behalf of the super fund, and is otherwise 'bare' of any other arrangements.

This arrangement continues while there is a borrowing in place. The bare trust needs to be removed when the loan is repaid, and the super fund then owns the property or shares outright. If the property or shares are sold, the bank loan is repaid first with any balance passing to the super fund.

If you have two properties and two loans in place, you need two bare trusts, as each of the property/borrowing arrangements is separate. The same goes with shareholdings in more than one company – for example, if you want to borrow to buy shares in three companies, that means three loans and three bare trusts.

Costs

Borrowing to invest through your DIY super fund is not an area where you can skimp on costs, as you need to get it right first time. There are costs involved with the bank, which will follow its own 'due diligence' process to ensure that your fund's trust deed allows you to undertake borrowing for the property or share investment, as well as ensure that the documents relating to the bare trust are all in order.

The bare trust needs to have a company as its trustee, and it's not legally possible to have the same company as trustee of your super fund as you have for the bare trust. The good news, if you have more than one borrowing arrangement, is that you can use the same company as trustee of each bare trust.

Get good legal advice

Finally, it's essential to get proper and complete legal advice to make sure that everything is done in the right order. Just to make it confusing, each state, for example, has a different set of requirements for the initial deposit on a property, the establishment of the bare trust and the transfer of loan funds. If these are done the wrong way round you could end up with a total mess, with the ownership of the property being in the wrong place at the wrong time, and the whole transaction then falling outside the law.

As well as the banking and legal costs, there are stamp-duty considerations in most states on the initial purchase of a property. Done properly, there should only be one payment of stamp duty at the time of purchase of the property by the super fund, and there should be no stamp duty at the time the borrowing is paid off and the property becomes fully owned by the fund, provided that the final settlement of the loan and the transfer of ownership of the property to the super fund are also undertaken properly.

Don't get caught out by not investing time and money in making sure that you have everything right. Considering the significant amount you are likely to be investing and what you expect to make from the investment in the future, you can't afford to be caught short by saving a few dollars on fees for professional advisers.

Allowing for the costs of borrowing and the need to get good professional advice, you will need to run the numbers to make sure that you will be better off under the borrowing arrangements compared to using borrowed funds outside super to undertake the investment or when buying the asset without borrowing (if that is financially possible). Make sure it works for you.

Don't forget life insurance

Property and shares are long-term investments, and most bank loans to super funds are for terms of 10 years or less, so it's important that you consider whether the loan will be repaid at that time or rolled over.

You need to think about what will happen to the loan if you or another principal member of the fund dies or is unable to keep working. For example, would the fund be able to keep up with the interest payments and be able to repay the loan on its maturity? For example, what if the investment was intended as a long-term asset to be retained within the family, such as a commercial property used by the family business?

In these cases, consideration needs to be given to arranging insurance on the life of the principal member or other members of the fund. Insurance will enable the remaining members of the fund to repay the bank loan and have enough cash to pay out the death benefits, while still retaining the property or shares in the fund.

You have to plan ahead and look at the exit strategy with any of these long-term investment and borrowing strategies.

Inside or outside super?

Don't be overwhelmed by the noise from promoters, banks and real estate agents about borrowing inside super. You need to check your reasons for considering borrowing inside super and make sure that this is the best place for you.

There are restrictions on the property investments that your super fund can purchase (with or without borrowing), and under super rules it is not permissible for you to live in a residential property while it is owned by the super fund.

There are also limitations on what you can do with the super-fund property that has been bought with borrowed funds, and these restrictions are imposed both by the law and by the banks that lend the money.

If you intend to make major changes to the property to improve it, you can't use the borrowed funds to do that – you need to use other super-fund cash. Since the property belongs to the super fund, it's important that bills relating to the property are paid from the fund and not by you personally.

Banks have generally stayed away from lending to super funds to buy vacant land, as the land will not lead to immediate rental income for the fund. They like to see regular income coming from the property to help meet the borrowing costs.

Remember that super funds are taxed at a concessional rate of no more than 15% on their investment income and no more than 10% on realised capital gains (when the asset is held for more than 12 months). This means that any borrowing costs are deductible to your super fund at a maximum of 15%. This compares to the deduction that you can get outside super, which is at your personal marginal tax rate.

So you need to consider the additional tax advantage that you can get with these deductions at the same time as thinking about the higher capital gains tax you might pay if the property is held outside super. It's essential you plan this through and see which approach might give you the best outcome before you get too far down the track with the borrowing-in-super strategy. Do your homework and choose what you think works best for you financially and personally.

If you're comfortable with property as an investment, then using your super fund to borrow to achieve an enhanced return on your capital is worth a good look. That said, always be aware of the exit strategy and consider how the property or shares fit within your overall investment strategy, both inside and outside super.

CHAPTER 8

Investment strategies and philosophies

It's your super fund, it's your super money, and it's your responsibility to make sure that it's invested wisely and appropriately to meet your goals. You are responsible for your own investment decisions. Much has been written about investing, and in this chapter it's only possible to touch on some of the key points as they relate to your super fund. It's important that you set the rules you intend to follow for investing your super money, and you need to stick to those rules.

Setting the investment strategy for your super fund

The law requires that, as a trustee of your super fund, you determine an appropriate investment strategy for the investment of the money inside your fund. This serves more than one purpose.

First, it keeps the fund's auditor happy, as they need to ensure that the fund has a documented investment strategy that shows the trustee has considered the key issues of risk, return, liquidity and diversification (each of which we will touch on below). The auditor will also look to ensure that you are investing the assets of the fund consistently with the stated investment strategy. The law also requires that the fund's investment strategy must also consider the insurance needs of the members of the fund, so don't forget to address that as well.

Second, the investment strategy should confirm to you what you are looking to achieve with the investment of your super money, and how you will do that. It's a bit like setting a New Year's resolution (one which you intend to keep!) about how you will invest your super-fund money. You should hold yourself accountable to the investment strategy and review your performance over time.

When you are investing your super fund's money, you not only need to set and follow an investment strategy, but you need to do so within the rules. Let's have a look at some of the rules and strategies that you should follow when investing your super money.

1. Know the law

We have already spoken about the two types of rules that apply to your super fund: superannuation law and your fund's trust deed. When investing you need to make sure you don't fall outside these rules.

If you invest outside the law and get caught (which you will), you will lose some of your hard-earned investment income and capital in tax and penalties. Don't be tempted to take the chance, even if it appears that there is no other solution. It's important to either take time to know the rules and how to stay within them, or arrange for a professional adviser to assist you with the investment process.

2. Investing directly into the market or using professional managers

You need to consider whether you have the time and appropriate expertise to assemble and maintain the fund's ongoing investment portfolio. If you think you would like help with that, there are a range of options available to you, from supplementary advice right through to using professional managers to manage parts of your fund's portfolio.

You might be comfortable with investing your portfolio and you might want occasional advice on parts of the portfolio, such as which company shares to buy, hold or sell. You can work with a stockbroker on these issues, and you can pay for their services either through a portfolio fee or when you take their advice to buy or sell shares.

Within the share investments, you can invest in what are called 'listed investment companies' (LICs), the most well known of which include AFIC, Argo Investments and Milton Corp. These companies invest across the total Australian share market, generally in line with the overall market index. As a result, you end up with your own share portfolio that is invested across all of the major Australian companies, but you don't need to worry about the detail. Half-yearly dividends are paid to you and these can be reinvested back into your LIC shares to keep your investment going over the long term.

If you want to step back from some of the more complex investment processes, you can select managed portfolios or managed funds within your super fund's portfolio.

If you are looking for an investment that covers the major investment sectors (Australian shares, overseas shares, property, fixed interest and cash), this can also be achieved by investing through managed funds. You buy units in the managed fund and the professional manager then combines your money with other unit holders' money to buy assets inside the managed fund. You end up with a broad portfolio, with the daily investment decisions being taken by the professional manager.

It's up to you how actively you want to be involved in the investment process for your super fund's money. The greater the level of involvement of outside parties, the higher your costs. But you might be prepared to put up with higher costs if you can leave the difficult investment decisions to others.

3. Buying assets from the market or transferring ownership

Your investment strategy will confirm the types of assets in which the fund can invest, but it will not dictate how the assets come into the fund.

In most cases, such as listed shares or property, you will buy the assets on the open market. There are some types of assets, commercial property and listed shares being examples, that can be bought from a person or business related to you, or that can be used as an in-specie contribution for you or other members of the fund. An in-specie contribution is useful if the fund does not have sufficient cash to buy the shares or property.

You will need to be careful with the annual super contribution limits that apply. If you exceed these limits you will be hit with penalty tax. If in doubt, get professional advice before undertaking any type of in-specie contribution to the fund.

In all cases, assets that are purchased from related parties or used to make an in-specie contribution must be transferred on a market-value basis. In the case of property, a formal valuation undertaken by an independent valuator is often required to validate the value at which the transfer or contribution was made.

4. Investing with a long-term strategy

Investing is a long-term game, so you should not be influenced by short-term distractions. You are running your own super fund because you want to take an interest in investing your own money, so you need to understand what your portfolio is doing along the way. And you might want to make adjustments to the portfolio from time to time.

If you are investing in listed shares, don't panic when markets decline. It's important that you show strength and use this as an opportunity to buy, if you have the spare cash to do so.

You should expect to have a stable core portfolio of investments and perhaps a small segment in which you undertake short-term trading (with or without stockbroker advice). However, you should restrict the portion of the fund that is actively traded to a small proportion, such as 5% or up to 10% of the total share portfolio, for example.

If you are confident you can correctly anticipate opportunities of investing better than the professional stockbrokers and investment managers, then trading in shares might be your game. However, this can take up a large part of your personal time and involve emotional wear and tear on you and your family. It's up to you to decide if you want to play on this roller-coaster.

Most importantly, always respect your super money, even though it is locked away until retirement. That's no excuse to gamble with your money and speculate rather than invest – there's a big difference.

5. Your strategy does not change in retirement

There's a lot of discussion out there about how to adjust your investment approach as you age. Be careful about what you see the retail and industry funds doing with their 'default' investment options.

A number of these funds use as their default strategy an 'age-based' portfolio, which reduces the growth asset portion as members age. Finally, at age 60, the default investment portfolio has a large proportion in more conservative fixed-interest and cash assets, and less in the growth-type assets such as shares and property. The reasoning is that at 'retirement age' (that is, age 65), they expect their members to be fully invested in cash in their super balances and they don't want you to be exposed to investment market risks at that time.

Is this what you intend to do with your own super fund? Cash it all in when you reach age 65? Probably not – it's more likely you will want to continue to actively invest during your post-retirement years for the long term.

How long is the long term? When you reach age 65, the average remaining life expectancy is another 20–25 years, and you should be looking at your investment portfolio as if you were investing over that period of time. Obviously, if your retirement balance is small relative to your annual pension payments, the period over which the capital will last will be shorter.

We'll talk later about how to structure your portfolio to allow for short-, medium- and long-term needs, and how these will change as you get older.

Let's have another look at Figure 4.1 introduced in Chapter 4, which was used to illustrate the three phases of your superannuation account, being accumulation (contribution), drawdown (but still growing) and drawdown (declining). You will see that most of the action occurs in the drawdown (post-retirement) period.

Figure 4.1: Superannuation Balance Across a Lifetime

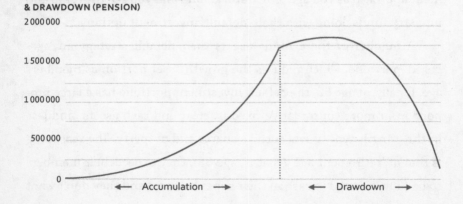

If you are an average person, over 60% of the total pension drawing that you will make over your post-retirement lifetime is funded from the investment income you earn after retirement. Another 30% comes from investment income earned prior to retirement, which means that only 10% comes from contributions. This shows the importance of the investment process post-retirement. You can't afford to take your foot off the pedal just because you have retired.

6. The importance of income

Don't forget the importance of income from your investments. The media constantly focuses our attention on what the share market is doing each day, and it's easy to get distracted from the income side of things.

The price of shares varies on a daily basis, even though the underlying dividend payments remain unchanged day by day (they get changed perhaps once or twice a year). We expect that over time the value of shares should increase, even though the road to growth is a bit rocky – but the flow of dividends will continue in the meantime.

If you are in retirement and paying yourself a pension, the income from your investment portfolio is important. If your investment income is more than sufficient to cover any super pension payments, or you are yet to start your super pension, you might consider whether to arrange for the reinvestment of dividends or distributions that your fund receives.

A large number of listed company shares offer investors the opportunity for 'dividend reinvestment' plans, under which the dividend that is paid is automatically used to buy more shares. By using dividend reinvestment, it is possible to achieve significant growth in the value of your portfolio without incurring brokerage on the take-up of the new shares.

The level of understanding that Australians have about shares has increased significantly over the last few decades, as has our involvement in the share market. Thirty years ago, less than 5% of Australians owned shares. As at the end of 2012, 38% of Australians owned shares, either directly or through managed funds, including through super.[1]

In Australia we are spoilt with the high dividend return we can get from our shares, with dividend yields up to 5% or 6% (before allowing for tax) being available in stable market conditions. In less favourable economic times, when market values are down, dividend yields could be as high as 7% or 8% (before allowing for tax). This compares to international shares, such as US stocks, which pay few or no dividends and have yields of no more than 2%, with no tax advantage to follow.

7. Investing with tax in mind

We have spoken earlier about the concessional tax treatment that super funds have in Australia, with a reduced rate of tax applying to investment income – 15% is a pretty good top rate of tax to be paying on investment income for your super fund. When making investment decisions for your super money, it's important you understand the impact that tax can have on the return from your investments.

A lot of information is presented in the media about the 'zero tax' environment that applies when a super fund is being used totally to support pensions for its members. Zero tax means no tax on investment income and no tax on capital gains that are realised when assets are sold.

But zero tax doesn't mean you can't take greater advantage of the tax system. In Australia we have a taxation system that generally

---

1 2012 Australian Share Ownership Study, published by ASX (Australian Securities Exchange).

applies tax only once to company profits and income. When you receive a dividend from an Australian company share, that dividend is paid out of the company's profit after tax has already been taken out. To avoid taxing that profit again, the dividend comes with an in-built credit called a 'franking credit', which is added back to the dividend when your super fund determines the tax that is payable.

If your super fund is fully supporting pensions, this means that a franking credit that comes from a company that is paying tax at the full rate (30% at the time of writing) will be worth an additional $30 for each $70 of dividend received.

Not only do you pay no tax, but your super fund is entitled to claim these franking credits back from the Tax Office as a refund of tax. If your super fund is fully supporting pensions, for every $100 of dividend received you can receive an additional $42.85 of tax credit, which gives you almost a 43% tax bonus.[2]

That is one of the reasons why our super funds find Australian shares so attractive as an investment, since the dividends can be worth more after tax than they were before tax. It's better to have shares inside your super fund rather than outside the super fund and taxed at around 47 cents in the dollar (before any franking credits are applied), for example.

If you expect to sell large assets that have given you a significant growth in value since you bought them, selling them when the fund is paying pensions will mean you pay no capital gains tax. Planning when to sell assets can give you a better outcome than just doing it without any planning.

---

2 You can work through this yourself by considering what happens when the company in which your super fund owns shares makes a before-tax profit of $142.85, and loses 30% of this as tax to the government (that's tax of $42.85). When your fund receives the resulting (after-tax) dividend payment of $100, it carries with it the credit for the tax of $42.85 that has already been paid by the company.

There's no doubt that how you structure your investment portfolio through the various life stages of the super fund is influenced by the effect of tax. Making the most of this comes down to understanding the effect of taxation and investing tax efficiently.

8. Using 'time profiling' to set up your investment portfolio

It's a bit too simple to think of your investments as being for one purpose only, as there are various stages for which you need to consider investing. While you might not want to go to this level of detail, it's worth looking at a concept called 'time profile' investing.

Let's consider that your super fund might have four stages for which you are investing.

(i) 'Now' (specifically, 0–2 years out from now)

What is the short-term budget for your super fund? What do you think you will pay out from your super fund over the next two years? This would include the next two years of pension payments and any additional benefit payments that might be made over that time. Insurance premiums, taxation and fund expenses need to be paid when they are due.

You need a short-term cash pot to meet these outgoings, and you need to feel confident that you can meet these without selling down investments. This is about understanding and managing your fund's liquidity.

If your fund is receiving contributions, you could allow for the net inflow from these when setting your 'liquidity pot'.

Short-term liquidity need not be achieved just by holding cash in the bank, as you can also use term deposits from quality banks and financial institutions for terms of up to 12 months within this 'liquidity portfolio'. It just needs to be accessible quickly if required.

If you are paying pensions from your cash holding, it's likely that dividends will be paid into the fund's cash account and not reinvested, which will improve the liquidity position.

(ii) Short-term future (2–5 years out from now)

Having secured your short-term liquidity position, what can you do to provide a layer of protection for the next few years? What can you fall back on if there is an extended economic downturn or stagnation and investment values and returns remain depressed for some time?

You don't want to be selling down your shares, property or other growth-type investments at a time when their value is below par. Ideally, you want to be doing the exact opposite: buying low and selling high (which is much easier said than done). To avoid selling low, this second tier of investment needs to be available to be called on if required.

This part of your portfolio requires a bit more patience in accessing, as it might not have the same immediate liquidity as the 'Now' part of the portfolio. It might involve, for example, term deposits with a term longer than 12 months, or fixed-interest or 'hybrid' investments from companies. These types of investments will fluctuate in value over time according to market conditions, but can generally be cashed in (sometimes at a discount to face value).

(iii) Long-term future (5 years plus from now)

This is the part of the portfolio that you do not expect to touch for a period of at least five years, with the first two stages being self-supporting, with dividend and other income (from investments and contributions) being used to top up the cash and liquidity part of the portfolio.

How do you want to invest the majority of your super money? This is the more complex part of the investment portfolio, as you need to try to match your investment portfolio to your attitude to risk. How much risk you want to take will determine the types of assets in the portfolio.

Generally, the higher the investment 'risk' you are prepared to take on, the higher the long-term return you should expect as recompense for that risk. Conversely, lower returns normally involve less risk. It's one of the fundamental principles of investing – and over most historical periods, this risk–return relationship tends to hold true.

Over an investment period of five years and more, investors are generally more tolerant of short-term market variations, as this part of the portfolio is not intended to be sold down for at least a further five years. By all means make changes within the portfolio to suit your longer-term investing goals, but don't try to make short-term judgements on where the market is going.

This part of the portfolio will include shares, both Australian and overseas, plus property and other 'growth'-type investments. Income from this part of the portfolio can be used to continually top up the 'Now' part of the portfolio.

(iv) Excess ('legacy')

It's not an exact science, but this part of the portfolio construction is about determining what you think might be more than what you need for you and your spouse/partner to live a comfortable life in retirement, with some room to spare.

This is the part of your super that you are investing for the benefit of the next generation – some might call it the 'legacy' portion of the portfolio. This is the part of your investment portfolio that is invested for the very long term, on the assumption that you will have a good life expectancy ahead. If you have a life expectancy of 10–15 years, for example, this part of the portfolio is not expected to be called on for another 10–15 years.

You might want to progressively involve your children in the investment decisions affecting this part of the portfolio, as they are likely to be the beneficiaries of this portfolio. The more that you can educate them on sound investment principles, the more confident you can be that they will be well equipped to invest any inheritance or legacy wisely.

> **SUPER TIP**
>
> Think about your own super fund and what you would budget to need in each of the four parts of the portfolio, based on your own circumstances.
>
> How do your current investments compare with the amounts you think you need according to your budget?

The types of investments that you have in these different portfolio stages will be very different. In the short-term stages, the emphasis is on income and security of capital. In the longer-term and legacy stages, the emphasis is less on income and more on capital growth. The assets in these latter-stage portfolios would be held with a long-term outlook, without expectation of needing to sell down in the short term.

9. Managing liquidity

Before making an investment, consider its liquidity. How easily can the asset be sold? Check if there has been any problem with cashing in these types of investments in the past. Is there an available market on which the asset can be cashed or sold? If there is no guaranteed market, you will need to factor this into the price you are prepared to pay for the asset and also where it fits into the 'time profile' portfolio stages.

That's where managed funds can be useful as compared to direct investing, as managed funds generally are much more able to cope with internal liquidity problems when some of the underlying assets may be compromised.

There is a lot of discussion about the virtues of property, but these can be totally overshadowed by losses that flow from a forced sale of the property if there is a need for urgent cash – for example, to make payment of a benefit on the death of a member of the fund.

That's why it's always useful to have an exit strategy for each major asset that the fund holds, to ensure that there is no need to undergo a forced sale at 'fire sale' prices.

That's also the reason for the four suggested stages of time-profile investing, to ensure that there is favourable liquidity for the short to medium term needs of the members of the fund – as summarised in Table 8.1.

Table 8.1: Four Stages of Time-profile Investing

TIME PROFILE	NOW	SHORT TERM	LONG TERM	LEGACY
Investment period	0–2 years	2–5 years	5–20 years	20+ years
How long can you wait for assets to be cashed if you sell them?	Immediate, up to 1 week	Up to 3 months	Less important	Less important
Can you afford to lose short-term value if you take higher risk for the long term?	No	Not a lot	Yes	Certainly

10. The importance of diversification

As well as liquidity, it's important to consider spreading your investments around. This is called 'diversification', which means avoiding putting all of your eggs in the one basket.

You can reduce your risk by spreading your money around and investing in different types of investments. This helps to protect your money, as it is unlikely that all of your investments will perform badly at the same time.

If you are unfortunate enough to be invested in a company or arrangement that goes under or into liquidation, you don't want to have all of your money locked up in that investment. No matter how good the return looks, it's not worth putting your whole life savings into a single investment. There are so many sad stories in the media of pensioners who have lost it all by investing their entire life savings in the one supposedly 'high-quality' investment that turns out to be a dud.

Spread your money around, across different types of investments and across different providers and companies. Make sure that you understand the nature of any 'guarantees' that are offered behind the investments – are they valuable guarantees, or are they not worth the paper they are written on?

If you do have a large property in your super fund, try to build up additional investments that will provide you with income and growth over time – which might come in handy if the tenants stop paying rent or the property is vacant for a time.

If you have a share portfolio, make sure you have a spread of shares across and within the different industry sectors, even if that means you might have shares in competing companies.

In Australia our share market is concentrated around financial and resources stocks, so it's worth having a look at your portfolio to see if it is sufficiently diversified across other industry sectors. The concentration of the Australian share market is one reason why having some overseas shares in your portfolio (either directly or through managed funds or exchange-traded funds) can be a good idea. By doing this, you can buy exposure to other business sectors that we just don't have in scale here in Australia, such as health care, information technology and telecommunications.

Achieving good diversification is possibly one of the hardest things to achieve with your super portfolio. But it's important to be thinking about it all the time, as you keep yourself accountable against your investment strategy and goals.

11. Be accountable to yourself

We spoke earlier about having an investment strategy that sets out the way you intend to approach investing your super-fund portfolio. It's important to keep on track with your investing and monitor your performance to make sure you are investing according to your agreed strategy.

But make sure you keep yourself accountable for how well you are investing your fund's money. Assess the returns you are earning on your fund over different time periods. Remember that you are investing for the long haul, so look at what you are achieving over periods such as 12 months, two years and three years, for example, rather than what you earned last month.

You should also consider comparing your fund's performance against some neutral benchmarks. By all means compare the performance against index changes, such as the Consumer Price Index (CPI), to determine the real rate of return you are producing by your efforts. You also need to compare the performance against alternative investments, such as specific managed funds that you could use within your super fund if you chose to do so. Make sure that these managed funds or portfolios are similar in their risk profile to your super portfolio, to ensure a 'like for like' comparison.

But if the return that your super fund is making is significantly less than the return from these alternative investments, you need to ask yourself why you may be wasting your time with this investing game when you can give the money to the experts to do better. Hopefully the return from your super portfolio will be comparable to or better than the returns from these alternative investments, and you can feel pleased with the results of your labours.

12. Will you have enough?

How long will you live and how long will your super last? There is increasing attention being given to these questions as our general health continues to improve. Don't just assume that you will live to the average life expectancy – add a few more years to allow for living beyond the average.

The issue of how much money you need to live in retirement was raised in Chapter 1, with $56 000 often quoted as the annual amount that (statistically) will support a comfortable retirement for an average couple. For a single person, it's $41 000 per annum.

Using the rule of thumb suggested in that chapter, a 60-year-old couple will need about $15 today for each $1 of annual income required in retirement – so this means that you might need around $850 000 set aside to secure your 'comfortable' retirement. Of course, that figure is based around averages. If you want to include a bit of extra 'stretch', just in case you plan on living longer than average, you could use a multiplier of not 15 but 17 (an addition of two years). That would then call for not $850 000 but $960 000 in retirement savings, for example.

These amounts can only be used as a guide to how much you will need to support your required lifestyle in retirement, without needing to call on the age pension for any of that support. Don't forget that the age pension will always be there as a safety net, but it's likely to become harder to obtain and less generous as the Australian population continues to age and greater pressures are put on the public purse.

Probably more important than your actual life expectancy is your 'mentally active' life expectancy. While Australians are living longer, more and more people are experiencing wear and tear on their mental faculties, with age-related diseases like Alzheimer's and dementia becoming more prevalent.

If you have your own super fund, how long will you be both interested and able to run the fund before it all becomes too hard? That's why it's important to gradually involve family and children in the running of your fund so that they can continue to run it and manage the investment portfolio that you have built up over the years. It's all part of the long-term management of your super fund.

Investing is a responsibility

These investment strategies make for a lot to think about, but most come down to common sense. If you approach the investment process carefully and have a plan, you will find that the responsibility of investing is not an onerous one. It's your super money and it's worth spending the time to feel comfortable with investing. You've got a long time ahead, and well-invested super will help you live the life you want to live.

CHAPTER 9
Super strategies

There's a lot you can do with your super, so it's important that you know how or where to get information and advice about some of the strategies worth considering. Most super strategies are about improving your after-tax outcome, which is quite a legitimate objective. I'll touch on a few of the more popular strategies in this chapter, with the aim of showing what you can do with your super. They include:

- claiming personal super contributions as tax deductions
- reducing the tax bite on your super after age 60
- improving the value of your death benefits
- borrowing to enhance value
- investing in business property or equipment.

Claiming personal contributions as tax deductions

Anyone can make their own contributions to superannuation if they are yet to turn 65, regardless of whether they are employed, self-employed or not working at all. After the age of 65, you need to be able to confirm that you have worked for at least 40 hours over a 30-day period before you can make contributions in that financial year.

Generally, if your employer is making contributions for you or if you are making salary-sacrificed contributions, you can't get any tax advantage from any of your own contributions that you make to super. If you are self-employed and don't have an employer making contributions for you, then the contributions you make to super are eligible for claiming as a personal tax deduction.

Why would you bother with this? Well, it's quite simple and comes down to managing the tax that you pay.

If you are fortunate enough to be earning income that results in you paying 47 cents in the dollar on your last dollars of income, then making a tax-deductible contribution to super will help you to reduce the overall tax you are paying.

If you make a $25 000 personal contribution to super and you are eligible to claim this as a deduction against your income, the $25 000 will be taxed at 15% inside your super fund, leaving you with $21 250 to invest in super. (That's $25 000 less the 15% contributions tax of $3750.) If you had taken the $25 000 as wages, you would have paid tax of $11 750, leaving net take-home wages of $13 250. If you can do without the money now (and get the benefits later), it's a 'no-brainer' to follow this strategy.

If you are running your own super fund and want to make these personal deductible contributions, make sure you take care of the proper documentation[1] that confirms that the contributions were being claimed as deductible contributions. If you're not sure if you're eligible to claim a tax deduction for any personal super contributions, talk to your adviser or tax agent before you make these contributions.

---

1 Section 290-170 of the Income Tax Assessment Act 1997 talks about the special documentation that must be completed, retained and provided to members to ensure that the contributions are properly recorded for tax purposes.

Reducing the tax bite on super after age 60

Reaching your 60th birthday is a major event for your superannuation. For the majority of us (with the exception of those in some public-sector super funds), we pay no tax on pensions or benefits taken from our super accounts after we turn 60. That's a pretty good outcome, and you should ensure you take advantage of it while it lasts.

Chapter 2 in part covers the privileges provided when a fund is paying pensions. Essentially these privileges mean that there is no tax payable on investment income or realised capital gains when your fund is only supporting pension accounts. It's therefore not surprising that there is a flurry of activity when people turn 60, and turn their DIY funds into pension-paying funds – not because they suddenly have a need for the pension payments that must be made from the pension accounts, but because the funds are free from tax on investment income and on realised capital gains.

Remember that you don't need to be retired to start a pension after you have reached your 'preservation age' – you can take a 'transition to retirement' pension if you are yet to turn 65.

After age 60, any pension payments are not subject to tax and you only need to make pension payments of 4% of the account balance each year. This means that for each $100 000 of your pension balance, you need to pay out a pension of at least $4000 in the year. Considering that you will pay no tax on that $4000, it's a pretty good outcome.

If your fund is earning investment income of 5% for each $100 000, you will have investment income of $5000, which will result in investment tax of $750 (being 15% of $5000). However, after age 60, by using a pension in your super fund you can save that tax of $750 for each $100 000 of balance, with no downside.

And if you don't need the additional income from the pension, you can always contribute it back to the super fund, provided that you have not already made contributions at the maximum level.

You can see from this simple example why using pensions after age 60 is a popular super strategy.

Improving the value of your benefits on death

No one really likes to talk about what will happen after they die, but this is an important issue for superannuation. While you and your spouse might pay no tax on your benefits or pensions after you reach the age of 60, the same can't be said for your children when they inherit your super benefits on your death. Sure, you can take out all of your super before you die, which avoids this tax. But what else can you do about this death tax?

Our tax system imposes a tax of 15% plus Medicare levy on the taxable part of your death benefits if they are paid to someone other than your spouse, your dependent children under age 18 or people who were financially dependent on you at the time of your death. In most cases, children over age 18 would not be classified as being financially dependent (even though you might be forgiven for thinking otherwise!).

It's unfortunate that we still have some form of death duties in Australia, but ordinarily there is no escaping tax on death benefits paid to mature-aged (independent) children. The fact is, though, that there is some escape, but it requires sufficient time to plan and achieve some improvement.

Let's take a quick refresher on how your super balance builds up over time:

- your employer makes contributions (compulsory or salary-sacrificed) for you
- you make personal contributions on your own behalf
- you make personal contributions and claim these as deductible
- your balance earns investment income and returns.

These are the main items that affect how your balance grows. Any personal contributions you make (and that you don't claim as a tax deduction) are added to what is called the 'tax-free component' of your balance. The 'tax-free component' will never be subject to tax when it is paid to you as a benefit in the future.

The remaining balance is called the 'taxable component', and this portion of your benefit is subject to tax if it is paid to you before age 60 or paid as a death benefit.

If all of your account was sourced from your employer's super contributions and investment earnings, you would have a balance that was 100% taxable component. This will not have any tax effect for you or your spouse if you receive benefits after your 60th birthday, but it will result in tax being deducted from your balance when it is paid to your mature-aged children or estate after your death. For each $100 000 of death benefit, that could be a tax of $16 500 (with a tax rate of 15% plus 1.5% Medicare levy) for example. That won't affect you, but it will impact your children!

Is there anything you can do to reduce this tax impost? The answer is a clear yes, but you need to consider whether there is any cost that you will incur to achieve this improved position for your children. Remember that it's unlikely to have any favourable effect on you, since you are not paying any tax on benefits or pensions after age 60 anyway.

The strategy that is followed to improve your tax position on death is called a 'withdrawal and re-contribution' strategy, since it involves withdrawing funds and then putting them back as contributions.[2] Since you need to withdraw funds, you need to be eligible to

---

2 While this strategy might sound a bit like a tax dodge, it has been given the thumbs up by the regulator, since it's possible that the tax might only be saved on death. If you use up your entire super before you die, then the withdrawal and re-contribution strategy will not reduce your tax if you only take your benefits after age 60.

receive benefits from your super balance. This means that you must have either met a 'condition of release' (see Chapter 2) or started a transition to retirement pension.

This is best illustrated by an example under which you have two accounts in different super funds. In the first fund, you have a balance of $500 000, which is fully taxable, having been sourced only from employer super contributions and investment earnings. You have an account with a nil balance waiting in the second fund. Your death benefit of $500 000 would incur tax of $82 500 (at 16.5%) if it is paid to independent mature-aged children.

After age 60, you draw $150 000 in a year from your account in the first fund and make a personal (non-deductible) contribution of $150 000 to your account in the second fund. As a result, at the end of this year you have two balances in the two funds totalling $500 000, but with a tax-free amount of $150 000 in the second fund. Your death benefits of $500 000 would incur tax of $57 750 (at 16.5% on $350 000) if paid to independent mature-aged children. This is an improvement of $24 750 for your children.

If this 'withdrawal and re-contribution' strategy is followed year after year, the outcome develops as shown in Table 9.1:

Table 9.1: Withdrawal and Re-contribution Strategy over Five Years

START OF YEAR	BALANCE IN FUND 1 (ALL TAXABLE)	BALANCE IN FUND 2 (ALL TAX FREE)	TAX PAYABLE ON DEATH (AT 16.5%)
1	$500 000	Nil	$82 500
2	$350 000	$150 000	$57 750
3	$200 000	$300 000	$33 000
4	$50 000	$450 000	$8250
5	Nil	$500 000	Nil

A number of things need to be in place for this strategy to work effectively.

First, as discussed earlier, it's important that there is no cost incurred by you in arranging the withdrawal and re-contribution. If there is, it means that you are spending some of your money today for the possible benefit of your children in the future.

Second, you need to have the $150 000 – or whatever amount that is to be withdrawn – sitting in cash and available for the transaction. If you are fully invested, you might not want to be selling investments to improve your children's tax position, as you might lose out by not being invested for a time – say, during a strong share-market run.

The example has been made simple to illustrate the favourable outcome for your children of the withdrawal and re-contribution strategy. You should talk to your trusted adviser before proceeding with these actions to ensure not only that you are doing it properly, but also that you do it as effectively as possible and don't incur any unnecessary tax (such as tax on contributions above your annual tax concessional limit).

By the way, if you are wondering why the example above used a $150 000 super contribution, this is the maximum contribution you can make with your own after-tax money in any one year. That said, don't forget you can contribute up to $450 000 in one go in a period of three consecutive years, as discussed earlier. In practice, this means you can do the withdrawal and re-contribution actions in bigger chunks if you are under age 65.

Borrowing to enhance value

Chapter 7 covered the use of borrowed funds within super to purchase property or shares. It's worth a reminder about the value you can get from using borrowed funds to invest, as well as the areas of risk.

If you have $100000 to invest, you can buy $100000 worth of shares. Over time, these shares pay you dividends of (say) $5000 per year, and increase in value from $100000 to $150000 over five years. During that period, you have received income of $25000 and achieved a gain of $50000 – a total net return of $75000.

Consider the situation if you had borrowed $200000 and used that together with your $100000 to buy $300000 worth of shares. Over that five-year period you would have received dividends of $15000 per year and your total share portfolio would have increased in value to $450000. If you had borrowed at an interest cost of 10% per annum, over the five years you would have paid interest of $100000, received income of $75000 and achieved a capital gain of $150000 – a total net return of $125000.

By using borrowed funds, under this set of circumstances the return has been magnified from $75000 to $125000, as summarised in Table 9.2.

Table 9.2: Borrowing to Invest in Shares that Increase in Value

	NO BORROWING	WITH BORROWING
Your own money	$100000	$100000
Borrowed money	Nil	$200000
Value of shares purchased	$100000	$300000
Final value of shares	$150000	$450000
Interest paid	Nil	($100000)
Repay borrowing	Nil	($200000)
Net gain in value	$50000	$50000
Dividends received	$25000	$75000
Overall return	$75000	$125000

However, borrowing to invest does not always work out. Let's look at what would have happened if the shares had reduced in value. If the $100 000 (un-geared) portfolio had reduced in value from $100 000 to $80 000, the total return over the five-year period would have been $5000 ($20 000 capital loss against $25 000 income). However, the borrowing strategy would have produced a total (net) loss of $85 000 ($160 000 capital loss against $75 000 income). In this case, the use of borrowed funds has magnified the loss from a small profit of $5000 to a loss of $85 000, as summarised in Table 9.3.

Table 9.3: Borrowing to Invest in Shares that Reduce in Value

	NO BORROWING	WITH BORROWING
Your own money	$100 000	$100 000
Borrowed money	Nil	$200 000
Value of shares purchased	$100 000	$300 000
Final value of shares	$80 000	$240 000
Interest paid	Nil	($100 000)
Repay borrowing	Nil	($200 000)
Net loss in value	($20 000)	($160 000)
Dividends received	$25 000	$75 000
Overall return	$5000	($85 000)

Proponents of borrowing as an investment strategy acknowledge that borrowed funds should not be used for the total available investment portfolio only the portion that is available for longer-term investment. As a result, any temporary decline in capital values can be ridden out, during which time the remainder of the portfolio can provide support and income for the investor.

Using borrowed funds within super is no different, and you should seek proper guidance to ensure that you fully understand both the rewards and the risks that go with the use of borrowed funds to enhance value within your super fund.

Investing in business property or equipment

We've spoken before about the almost unlimited options you have for investing your super fund's assets, provided the investment is consistent with the fund's investment strategy and has a genuine investment purpose.

Property is one of the most common assets used in DIY funds, and that's not surprising when you consider that self-employed people and small-business owners represent a significant portion of DIY fund operators. Investing in your own business premises can make sense, even more so if you use your super fund to hold the property.

The lease payments that the business makes to occupy the property are made to the super fund and are taxed at 15% (at the most) and nil (at the lowest), which is likely to be a much better rate of tax than if the property was held personally or through a trust structure (when it would be likely to be taxed at 30%).

But it's not just the business property that the super fund can hold as an investment. If your business uses special equipment and needs to lease that equipment from a third-party company, you could consider having your super fund buy the equipment and then lease it back to your business. The lease must be a proper commercial lease and you need to ensure that the business makes the lease payments on time and at the right rate. Holding the equipment as an asset of the fund again keeps the lease payments in the super fund and also retains the equipment as an asset of the fund.

This is just another example of using your super fund in a way that supports both the members of the fund and the business that you operate – a win-win outcome, using super to greater advantage.

I've touched on only a few of the strategies you can undertake using super and your fund to achieve a financial advantage along the way. It's a good idea to seek expert advice from a trusted adviser to ensure you don't miss out on some of these opportunities – and to investigate what super strategies may be available and suitable for your situation.

CONCLUSION

When contemplating life after full-time work it's easy to place greater focus on plans, cashflow and how we want to live than on detailed investment strategies. Clear long-term goals are admirable, but it's crucial to take action and implement plans to create wealth.

Like so many people, super is the second-biggest asset I own, and it will play a critical role in my future plans. I have to plead guilty to having my super in three separate places. My wife and I have a DIY super fund; I have my work super that started many years ago with one super manager; and now that the company I founded with my partners – ipac securities – is part of the AMP group, I also have new workplace super with AMP.

Yes, I know I should roll it all into one fund. But real life is rarely simple. My old work super provides me access to a fund with really, really low fees – in fact, they are basically non-existent. That said, I reckon I'll get around to rolling my old work-based super into my newer ipac employers' fund, and keep the DIY going. I am now 58 and pondering my future. Like most people, I'll have to keep working – the reality is that the potential of 30-plus years of retirement means I need to keep income coming in.

But as I consider my impending 60th birthday, I am very aware of the potential to convert my super to a pension fund, meaning it pays no tax on investments in the fund. This of course will depend upon what I am doing work-wise, but it is worth thinking about now.

The world is complex and will keep changing. The best way to handle change is to have your money and your investment vehicles such as super under control today, and to have a sound understanding of how they work now. Then changes will be much more easily absorbed.

I hope this book has helped inspire you to take charge of your super and equipped you with the necessary knowhow – because despite the fact that today there is a lot of good advice available to us, the simple truth is that no one cares more for our money than we do personally. Knowledge is our best defence to protect ourselves from major money disasters. Equally, knowledge is our best weapon when it comes to making good decisions.

ACKNOWLEDGEMENTS

Do it Yourself (DIY) super funds are now a major part of our financial landscape – so much so that I have wanted to write a book specifically on self-managed super funds for some time.

But I have to thank Lou Delfos, Executive Chairman at ipac south australia, and his colleague Peter Crump, for giving me the motivation and adding the specialist skills that this book needed. DIY funds are complicated beasts with significant legislative complexity. Sure, you can outsource this to competent professionals, but it seems to me that if you are going to start up a DIY fund, the name alone should give you a bit of a hint.

If you have no interest in getting involved, why would you go down the DIY route?

Readers of this book will know I have a DIY fund with my fellow member and trustee, my wife Vicki. We are deeply interested in our money so 'doing it ourselves' appealed to us, but what we found missing was a single source of information that not only helped us to do it ourselves, but enabled us to answer the first key question: is a DIY super fund right for me? I have no doubt some readers will indeed decide DIY super is not for them.

This book simply would not have happened without Peter Crump. His expertise in simplifying and explaining DIY super, and providing the key technical information and investment strategies, is at the heart of this book. I have greatly enjoyed writing along-side Peter. This book is his first experience of being a co-author. As an actuary he is obviously a man of high intellect and attention to detail, but the pressure of joining me in writing a book to a deadline is a little like undertaking a highly intense university course while you are doing a full-time job.

I would also like to thank my trusty colleague Chris Walker who once again has added his very special calm approach to meeting deadlines. Chris was responsible for taking my words and Peter's words and producing the book.

Special thanks also to Rachel Scully, my Penguin Executive Editor and Ben Ball, Publishing Director. We had a number of robust conversations about what Penguin would call my 'chatting at the pub' writing style. I rather like writing as I speak, and I was highly amused at the pub reference. I wish I had thought of that. Rachel has done a terrific job in keeping my personality through the edit process, while making the book flow a lot better. Mind you, pub talk often makes a lot of sense!

INDEX

accountant 87

accumulation phase of
    superannuation 130

accumulation super fund 34

administration, offences in 94–5

administration provider 87

advice and support 89

AFSL (Australian Financial Services
    Licence) 104

age
    access to pension 30–1
    at retirement 9–11, 30–1,
        145–6
    and risk-taking 5–6, 7
    Age Pension 2, 4, 30–1, 142

age-based portfolios 129–30

annual living costs 13

annual return 77, 91, 94–5

APRA *see* Australian Prudential
    Regulation Authority

arms-length basis 95

assessable income 25, 131–2

assets
    buying on open market 128

buying or transferring 96
    and death of a member 98
    fund with personal trustees 98
    as in-specie contribution 128
    purchased from related
        parties 128
    record-keeping 85, 97, 98
    separating from super 98
    transferring ownership 128
    when to sell 133

ASX300 41

audit 68
    by ATO 50–1, 91, 94–5
    common offences 93–9
    compliance-based regulation
        50–2, 66
    cost 86
    a fixed service 90
    a monitor of fund 91
    penalties 52

auditor 51, 66, 86, 91
    and investment strategy 125–6

Australian Prudential
    Regulation Authority 35